Religion as Anxiety and Tranquillity

Religion and Reason 5

Method and Theory
in the Study and Interpretation of Religion

MOUTON · THE HAGUE · PARIS

Religion as Anxiety and Tranquillity

An Essay in Comparative Phenomenology of the Spirit

by

J. G. ARAPURA

McMaster University

MOUTON · THE HAGUE · PARIS

This book has been published with the help of a grant from the Humanities Research Council of Canada, using funds provided by the Canada Council

Library of Congress Catalog Card Number: 74-184758

Jacket design by Jurriaan Schrofer

© 1972, Mouton & Co., Herderstraat 5, The Hague, Netherlands

Printed in Hungary

Preface

This work is an articulation of what has been one of the deepest interests of the author for many years; in fact it is the crystallization of a very extensive study. It has been thought advisable to publish this work in the condensed essay form in which it is as, for one thing, it has so come about that it fully expresses what the author wants to communicate and, for another, there has been mounting in his mind a certain impatience to share his thought with scholars and ordinary people around the world who have the same concern as he – and they may prove to be far more numerous than suspected.

It will be noticed that throughout these pages there lurks a desire to see (not necessarily in this work, but more likely in the work of others who may respond to it in due time) that comparative religion is built on a new foundation. In this work the tack followed has been to make comparative religion join the destiny of philosophy (in the genuine and everlasting sense and not in the petty sense with which 'philosophy' has currently come to be associated). But this path has its perils, most of all because philosophy itself has never been able to come of age. However, when philosophy realizes the (paradoxical) reason why, it can put on courage: like religion itself, it cannot come of age because it was born old. This common destiny must be suffered; even the picayuneness of some forms of philosophy is part of it.

In writing this, every effort has been made to use plain and simple language only, except where absolutely necessary, and to avoid professional jargon. It is hoped that the result is satisfactory.

The author shares the satisfaction which comes from the completion of this work with the one person in this world, who more than any others has helped to usher it in and has suffered with him and thought with him through all its stages, his wife, as she has known better than anyone else that this book expresses one of the profoundest concerns of the author in recent years.

J. G. Arapura

Contents

Introduction

This essay arises out of comparative religion but the matter it concerns has seldom been thought about, and in this author's knowledge never before articulated in the manner attempted here. That matter is exactly what the subtitle tells: a comparative phenomenology of the spirit (mind). But comparative religion is its foundation and springboard, as religions are the matrices of what we expect to compare, namely, some self-distinguishing and self-identical spiritual spheres in the world. As for the motive actuating this particular study, on the one hand there is a desire to make a philosophical response to a very important dimension of contemporary awareness, and on the other, there is a wish to see discussions in comparative religion rendered somewhat more existentially relevant, perhaps by throwing a different light on the subject.

But, as comparative religion is its solid foundation, from which alone it can spring forward, and without which it could not even possibly arise, we will and must begin with consideration of that discipline so as through it (and through it alone) to move directly to the matter that is being set forth. Accordingly, then, this essay will not move on the main course of comparative religion, as customarily understood, as it will become immersed in the related problems of a comparative phenomenology which comprehends wider areas of spiritual life than are ordinarily expressed by the word 'religion'.

In view, however, of the intimate and, in fact, dependent relation that this study has to comparative religion, adverting to that discipline would be a natural first step. The year in which this essay was begun, 1970, had special significance as far as comparative religion is concerned, in the sense that it was the centennial year of the formal inauguration – if one may speak of such a thing – of this discipline.[1] That, of course, must depend upon the view that one takes of the matter, but it is not crucial, being of merely symbolic significance. No doubt, this essay is itself intended as a contribution to comparative religion but concerned with areas not normally covered, areas of life and awareness that surround, have emanated from, and, perhaps in some ways, underlie the religions instead of the religions as such. Such areas are what we will call the spiritual spheres.

By turning to these spheres the purpose is not to turn away from the religions but to overcome the formal limitations associated with them in the shape of their histories, community structures, rites and doctrines relating to God, man, salvation, etc., in comparative study. Cognizance is taken of the fact that many spiritually concerned persons no more live, think or act within such formal boundaries. Yet through the character of their consciousness they still have living links with certain religions and may be even more deeply immersed in the spiritual questions embalmed in them than those who still subsist and function within their recognized bounds. Persons like Nietzsche and Heidegger, for instance, are certainly not spokesmen of Christianity as such but are nevertheless eminent spokesmen of that spiritual sphere of which Christianity is the historic, religious centre; and it would be absurd to exclude such men from a comparative study that aims to be really significant for today. The inquiry embodied in the following pages is consciously designed to face up to that situation. Furthermore, that budding but still largely incipient activity which has officially come to be called comparative philosophy cannot, unfortunately, effectively fill the role as, among other reasons, its range is still very narrow. It is hoped that a comparative phenomenology of the spirit can assist it to grow somewhat more vigorous as well as much larger in scope.

The three words of the subtitle, 'comparative', 'phenomenology' and 'spirit' really express the essence of the study. The importance of the first of these words in what purports to be a comparative study goes without saying, but some rather novel ideas pertaining to it will be put forward. The word which is central to the book is 'phenomenology'. Consciousness will be presented as the authentic subject-matter of phenomenological inquiry; but it will be presented both in its singular and differential senses. In the first, that is the singular, sense, phenomenology will concern itself with the problem of consciousness reflecting upon itself – to do so being consciousness's essential and inalienable character – the study of which will involve both descriptive and empirical methods. And also, as consciousness reflecting upon itself has got to do with religion, consideration of it will involve some aspects of the phenomenology of religion, which will undoubtedly call for the normative method. And in the second, that is the differential, sense it will concern itself with certain spiritual perceptions, awarenesses and expressions which will have to be seen in the light of some fundamental diversities, distributed along the same lines as the religions, being dependent on them. In terms of these we shall outline certain distinct spheres of spiritual life.

Therefore, beginning with the question of the self-reflection of consciousness, two different but closely related problems will be investigated. The first will call for the singling out and uncovering of a certain ultimate, self-constitutive and existential element of consciousness, by means of which a particular dynamic in the original manifestation (though not the origin as such) of religion will be made to reveal itself. This element of consciousness to be labelled 'the sense of the wrongness of existence', is to be thought self-constitutive rather than adventitious because we know consciousness now here apart from it. However, it is not put forward as the basis for a complete or all-sufficient explanation of the phenomenon of religious consciousness but only as a fundamental but insufficiently recognized factor that needs to be brought to light. By the same token, it will be pointed out that we cannot go far with the purely descriptive analysis of the sense of wrongness without linking it normatively with what actually has happened in the history of religion. The limitations in the approaches of pure descriptive phenomenology and even of existentialism will also have to be made apparent.

Now, history of religion, when the term is applied to actual states of affairs rather than to the discipline known by that name, must no doubt be expressed in the plural. There are, however, phenomenological and existential philosophers who have, by incorporating history of religion into their thinking, thought normatively, but unfortunately their norm has been the history of one religion, namely, Christianity, appearing openly in some and through garbled analogies in others. Therefore, it would seem imperative that type differentiation of the ways in which that fundamental element of consciousness, the sense of the wrongness of existence, expresses itself and works itself out in different religions be thoroughly considered. Nevertheless, as our purpose is not to give any kind of causal account of the differentiation in existential consciousness as such, even if such a thing were possible, there is no need to enter into the question of any general typology of religion or culture or any other phenomenon, in view of the self-imposed limitation of the essay. We may the better abide with the typology of consciousness itself, not, however, indeed with any intention to do the reverse, namely, to give a causal account of the differences among the religions, for which there is no call here. Perhaps there may be a reciprocal causal relation obtaining between the two, but matters of this kind – all causality questions in fact – clearly fall outside the purview of the phenomenology here being constructed. The different ways in which the aforementioned fundamental element of consciousness, the sense of wrongness, is apprehended, expressed and dealt with in different religions are also reflected in the different approaches to the spiritual life and thought manifested in whole spiritual spheres, cognate with those religions. Thus it will be established that the phenomenology of religion cannot be really developed without resort to a *comparative* phenomenology of religion, which in turn will require the study of existential consciousness. This fact itself may be pointed out as one explanation for the diversity of the religions. Every theory of the origin of religion speaks of a unitary origin, ostensibly applicable to all the religions. The fact of differentiation is usually accounted for in secondary ways, through history, geography and economics. But in this essay origin and differentiation are considered together with a view to showing that while, unquestionably, all religions have some common genetic foundations, the differences also go back to those very foundations.

It would become clear that the typology of consciousness can be grasped only in conjunction with different spiritual spheres which, it will be seen, though based on religions cognate with them, are larger, wider and more general in their sway. One of the implicit efforts of this essay is to demonstrate that these spheres are realities and that, furthermore, they have remained self-identical through large segments of known history, for as Marcus Aurelius has said, 'A sphere once formed continues round and true'.[2] This will bring us to the third word of the subtitle, 'spirit'. No caution can be too great in the use of this word, which is charged with a complexity of metaphysical connotations, not the least of all in the Hegelian philosophy. In the form of *Geist* it occupies the very centre of Hegel's system. The word is not used here in Hegel's sense, but this declaration should not involve us in an obligation to redefine what Hegel has elaborated so thoroughly and so grandly, for to undertake such an unwarranted responsibility within the space of a short essay like this would be sheer foolhardiness as well as presumption. Besides, the conception of this essay does not call for such an effort. All that is required is to clarify that the word is not used in the comprehensive, metaphysical sense in which it was employed by Hegel but rather as a substantive fashioned from the adjective 'spiritual', a reversal of normal linguistic procedures to be sure. And why 'spiritual'? The purpose is to show what makes the spheres spheres and what gives them unity and to show also the common grounds for mutually comparing them. It is to be taken therefore as principally more akin to what Hegel himself has called 'religious life' rather than to anything else, with the qualifications spelt out above, that is to say, without the intrusion of the formal boundaries of the religions but with the inclusion of factors that have sprung from, and lean upon, the religions. Then again, comprehensive descriptions or outlining of the spiritual spheres in their entirety is not intended. What is aimed at is simply to isolate significant samples that respond to existential queries.

In view of the limitation in scope and the intended direction of the essay, certain categories of existential consciousness connoted by the type words 'anxiety' and 'tranquillity' and such other pairs as readily perform the desired function, will be used as keys for the entry into two eminent spheres that will be engaged for analytical comparison. The method, therefore, will be one of exemplification of these spheres through these lead categories. This limitation of scope imposed upon the essay is not deemed a defect insofar as what is really sought after is keys to the spheres in question, which in turn by reason of their eminence represent the possibility of studying a wider list of spheres. The restriction of the spheres to the two particular ones that will be selected is primarily due to practical and historical considerations and whatever involvement of theoretical principles there is is simply *ex post facto*. By deliberate design much of this essay is intended to be a bilateral comparison between the two spiritual spheres based on Christianity and Hinduism–Buddhism respectively. One can at least say that these two are the most obvious ones in the horizons of spiritual awareness today; and these are engaged in some kind of implicit contest. Interest in Indian (or the vaguer and more general 'Eastern') spirituality is an increasingly conspicuous trait of some sections of Western intelligentsia in the present day, which may perhaps be due to the fact that in this age of mounting anxiety they hope to find sources of tranquillity elsewhere than in their accustomed sphere, quite regardless of the question whether such high expectations are likely to be fulfilled.

Now, the approach through comparison, phenomenology and the spirit must exhibit some palpable kinship with the philosophies of Kant, Hegel and Husserl, among others, which must forthwith be exposed. But then it is bound to become evident that instances of kinship are also points of departure from the great thought systems these men have espoused. Critical departures also often involve adaptations of methods and principles prominent in them. Kant's fundamental teaching on the characteristics of comparison, Hegel's programme of erecting philosophy on the foundation of religion, along with the comparing of the religions to that end, and Husserl's method of reflecting upon consciousness are the most obvious in the apparatus to be adopted. The use to which Kant's thought will be put consists in the incorporation of the principles of homogeneity and heterogeneity. In respect of Husserl it may be said in brief that: (1) phenomenology of consciousness will be guided exclusively through certain religious elements and therefore the use made of it will tend to be progressively less descriptive and more normative, and (2) it will be conceived and structured in a strictly comparative manner. In respect of Hegel the intriguing concept no doubt is spirit but in the following ways our approach will differ from his: (1) the concept of the spirit will be used in the sense of the 'spiritual', which will be really 'spirit' at the lower levels of its power; (2) the comparative approach will not be treated as merely provisional as though eventually to be transcended by the absolutist approach, but will remain true to itself from beginning to end. Now, by way of explanation, it must be added that in the course of finding one's passage along a new line of thought, critical departures from several other leading systems also will have had to be made, but such departures should not be construed as comprehensive criticisms of those systems, for even to give the impression of indulging in an undertaking of the kind in a brief essay like this is, to say the least, audacious.

The question may finally be asked, what is the real purpose of a comparative study such as this? It can be said to be twofold, firstly, pure human self-knowledge, and secondly, understanding of the spheres of the spiritual life that are actually there. As E. Cassirer rightly observes, in all genuine philosophies, both Eastern and Western, and in all religions, self-knowledge has been considered 'a fundamental obligation', 'a categorical imperative', 'an ultimate moral and religious law'.[3] Among philosophers Hegel must be given a place of distinction in that in the spirit's gigantic movement he saw the implicit goal of absolutist philosophy, which is self-knowledge, and he assigned to religion the central place in this movement. It is clear that nothing partial, piecemeal or occasional could serve this goal. If religion is considered just a phenomenon among phenomena then it will hardly warrant philosophical study. As the call of philosophy is to study necessary rather than accidental things,[4] religion has to be so interpreted as to fall within the former category, and it will automatically do so if its indispensability for self-knowledge can be demonstrated. These are by and large the implicit principles in Hegel's philosophical method and they ought to be there in any that seriously concerns itself with religion. In our method we will try to show the non-accidental but necessary character of religion, based on consciousness, which like being is what necessarily is. In respect of the understanding of the spheres of the spiritual life, the word 'dialogue' would become significant. Granted, it is a rather hackneyed and often misused word, with an optimistic and quite sentimental ring about it. But it will be used here only to indicate the deepest possible level of comparativel study. In that light it will be presented as an intrinsically intellectual, essentialy contemplative activity that each person will have to carry out for himself in the privacy of his thought and to be expressed through the vehicles of thought. Nevertheless, it will not be a subjective activity as the role of thought is to express the form of spiritual life as such and in its entirety, and in the dialogue situation it expresses that form as it exists in more than one sphere.

The thinker must bring about a dialogue in his own mind between the different spheres by his thinking them together. In every genuine comparative study of such phenomena as are being considered here, there ought to take place a mutual encompassing, of which dialogue must represent the highest moment. The notion of mutual understanding will have to be replaced by that of the understanding of two things (or spheres) in their essential mutuality. The law that underlies it is that each of these can be penetrated the better if the two are penetrated together. Thus it will eminently serve the purpose of philosophy and unveil the potential beginning of a sphere of spheres, which will, however, enternally call for a twofoldness of perspectives on all matters. The two spheres that will be outlined here will provide the twofold point of view indispensable for a complete approach to philosophical understanding. Each sphere by itself will, of course, in principle provide the twofold point of view in the sense of the combination of views from inside and outside. But the twofoldness of view based on one sphere alone will be forced to draw its substance from mere logical considerations rather than from the forms of actual spiritual life, and hence in a sense it is ultimately bound to become ethereal, which will not have to be the case if it is based on two really existent spheres.

Contrary to much present practice, the author will not employ the concept of dialogue between the religions, for there one does not really know what is being talked about. If an organized activity of communities is what is meant then it has little relevance and less philosophical significance. Nor can a conference of individual persons presumably representing the different religions have much meaning. Further, though churches may have representatives, it is hard to see how religions as religions can have them. If, contrary to all this, a purely philosophical activity is designated by 'dialogue', then the religions have to be placed in larger settings, namely corresponding spheres of the spirit. Dialogue philosophically should also be considered as an extension of the means of self-knowledge. In every act of self-knowing, what in Plato's words is called 'the dialogue of the mind with itself' or in Hegel's words called 'dialectic' must take place. In terms of the dialogue between the spiritual spheres the thinker must perform a rather complicated task of thinking together these already completed spheres of self-knowledge. He must send out his own mind like a hound to traverse the pathways through which the spirit has come to a knowledge of itself in those spheres. All this must sound somewhat like Hegel, to be sure. But this author parts company with Hegel when the latter seems to speak on behalf of, and even legislate for, the Spirit. Our assumption is that we cannot actually speak anything about the union of oneself and the other through the dialectical movement of the Spirit, but we can speak something about the dialogical encounter and even union of oneself with the other through human acts of thought. In brief, however, the comparative phenomenology of spirit, far from being unrelated to the quest for self-knowledge, rather underscores its gravity and complexity.

In this context, one other conspicuous instance of similarity between Hegel's philosophy and the thought unveiled in this essay must be clearly pointed out, which is in respect of the call of the thinker as the new priest. The difference, however, is that in this scheme the thinker will not be summoned to think Hegel's all-comprehending speculative philosophy, from above or from anywhere, but simply to think the different spheres together as it were horizontally. Such a priestly act is the chief goal to which this essay will seek to move, but that goal will also underlie the whole work.

The occasion to make one last observation has now come. Comparative religion has seldom been thought capable of contributing to the ends of philosophy, self-knowledge or any other. On the whole it has remained at the level of an applied discipline, not capable of generating principles of its own but using principles borrowed from other disciplines. This picture can and must be changed. In a real sense, Hegel's own ideas must be thought to have great potentialities for raising it from that state and placing it at a genuine philosophical level. That the higher vocation of comparative religion as a contributor to self-knowledge as well as to the more comprehensive aspects of knowledge that philosophy seeks can be realized is one of the arguments of this book. All this calls for an effort to recover comparative religion for philosophic thought. But that effort will have to be made in a very special manner here in the light of a particular view of philosophic thought envisioned in this work. However, it is freely conceded that other ways also exist for the same purpose, although we will, in the following pages, address ourselves to the task in our own way.

2

The Philosophical Scope of Comparing in Religion

This treatise entertains, as one of its principal objectives, it has already been made explicit, the possible re-establishment of a link once partially forged, but later seriously weakened, between comparative religion and philosophy; therefore, it behoves us to begin by considering the scope of comparing in some relevant philosophers, most important of all Hegel. And since this essay has been conceived in such a way as to abide within the limitations it has erected for itself there is no reason to go much behind that chosen station of departure, Hegel, whose thought on the subject will continually remain one of the main pillars upon which this edifice must rest.

The method of comparing for the sake of knowledge is not without some venerable antiquity. Aristotle maintained that there is no science of that which is unique. Among the modern philosophers who revived interest in the method of comparison, Immanuel Kant is the chief. It is true, no doubt, that Kant placed transcendental reflection above logical reflection for the reason that the latter 'is a mere act of comparison', a position that apparently belittles the value of such an act. However, the record will be set straight as we read soon thereafter that 'transcendental reflection which bears on the objects themselves contains the ground for the possibility of objective comparison of representations with each other'.[1]

Kant was much impressed with the need for 'concepts of comparison' and spelt it out thus: 'Before constructing any objective judgment we compare the concepts to find in them *identity* (of many representations under one concept) with a view to particular judgments, *agreement* with a view to *affirmative* judgments, *opposition* with a view to *negative* judgments, etc.'[2] Nevertheless, he made a distinction between the 'logical form' and the 'contents' of consciousness.[3] His discussion of this distinction may be paraphrased as follows: logical reflection can only assist in mere comparison *(comparatio)*, that is to say, of the logical form of concepts, not of concepts themselves, which call for transcendental reflexion *(reflexio)*. Its importance is expressed thus: 'Since the things can have a twofold relationship to our faculty of knowledge, namely to sensibility and to understanding, it is the place to which they belong in this regard that determines the mode in which they belong to one another.'[4]

Kant expanded the methodology of comparison through the pairs, identity-difference, agreement-disagreement, and matter-form. Of these the first pair represents a vital problem in both logic and metaphysics and has been recently re-examined by Heidegger in his studies on Kant.[5] But customarily, it has been employed solely for resolving metaphysical, or what Heidegger calls 'onto-theological',[6] questions, and therefore in a study such as this it can hardly be useful. The two middle pairs are far more relevant in that they can be drawn into phenomenological inquiries. Kant observes that reality as noumenal *(realitas noumenon)* will not allow opposition while, 'on the other hand, the real in appearance *(realitas phaenomenon)* may certainly allow opposition'.[7] Likewise, with respect to the *inner* versus *outer* he writes: 'In an object of pure understanding that only is inward which has no relation whatsoever (so far as its existence is concerned) to anything different from itself. It is quite otherwise with a *substantia phaenomenon* in space, its inner determinations are nothing but relations and is itself entirely made up of mere relations.'[8] It seems that Ernst Cassirer arrived at a very clear understanding of Kant's purpose, which was, according to him, to mediate between two groups of scholars and scientists, those who follow the principle of 'homogeneity' and those who follow that of 'specification' or heterogeneity. Kant, he argued rightly, does not regard these two attitudes as mutually opposed as they do not express any fundamental ontological difference. 'They rather represent', observes Cassirer, 'a twofold interest of human reason. Human knowledge can attain its ends by following both ways and by satisfying both interests.'[9]

Although Kant enunciated these above principles universally applicable to the comparative method, he did so only as part of a general theory of knowledge and nowhere undertook to employ them for any concrete phenomena including the religions. However, in the post-Kantian era some philosophers thought to apply comparison to the field of religion of whom the most outstanding are Schleiermacher and Hegel to whom, therefore, we must turn.

Let us consider Schleiermacher first. We must, however, distinguish between the earlier Schleiermacher, the author of *Reden (On Religion)* and the mature Schleiermacher who wrote *Der christliche Glaube (The Christian Faith)*. In *On Religion*[10] he was more interested in setting forth what religion is and communicating it to 'its cultured despisers' than in uncovering historical religions and much less in comparing them. But while it cannot be claimed that comparing the religions was by any means the major interest in *The Christian Faith* it certainly was one very visible interest. We see him, as a liberated theologian, pondering, like many others of his time, on the problem of 'natural religion', the essence of which was 'simply what can be abstracted from the doctrines of religious communions as being present in all but differently determined'.[11] 'Such a natural religion', he argued, 'would mark out the common elements in all religious affections which are found in all ecclesiastical communities ... and also of all philosophical systems as having adjusted their differences as regards the terminology of such doctrines.'[12] Here lies the source of Schleiermacher's concern with the comparative study of religion; but he himself understood it in only a rudimentary, although essentially philosophical, manner.

From Schleiermacher we must quickly move on to Hegel. Re-study of Hegel's works will reveal the depth of his interest in comparing the religions. That interest was based on the extremely important place he assigned to the historical religious actualities and the fact of there being such actualities in his understanding of philosophy. It was on these that the edifice of his whole system was founded. Emil Fackenheim, a distinguished scholar of this aspect of Hegel's thought, observes: 'Hegel holds the actual existence of religious life to be an indispensable condition not only (as is obvious) of his philosophical comprehension of religion, but also (as is far from obvious) of his philosophy as a whole.'[13] If we look closely and freshly we can find confirmation of this fact throughout Hegel's writings, as for instance where, typically, he stipulates, 'philosophy unfolds itself when it unfolds religion'.[14] Like Schelling, Hegel looked to a realm beyond reflective thought as the foundation for philosophy, with the difference, however, as Richard Kroner observes, that 'with Schelling this realm was poetry; with Hegel, religion'.[15] The relation between the absolute religion (Christianity) and the absolute philosophy (Hegel's philosophy) being the corner-stone of the whole system, the diversity of the religions was bound to offer him, as it did, a very serious intellectual challenge, and constituted a source of intellectual dilemma. Fackenheim sums up Hegel's dilemma very succinctly in the following words: 'Either Hegel's philosophy remains bound up with the religious basis it is said to require: but then (since there is no religion but only religions) must it not be confined to the limitations of one religion thus losing its claim to absolutism? Or else it preserves its absolutism, and renders each religion what may be its due: but is it not then cut off from its religious foundation, which is one specific religion? In either case religious life fails to furnish the bridge between finite life and infinite philosophical thought. Yet it is this bridge which we have found to be indispensable for the entire Hegelian philosophy.'[16]

Schleiermacher, a theological apologist for the Christian religion, was also faced with this dilemma although in a different way, and for different philosophical reasons, from Hegel. Both these thinkers found some scheme of comparing the actual historical religions of the world necessary. In the schemes they adopted are reflected their respective philosophical standpoints. In contrast to Hegel's, Schleiermacher's is a simple and cheerfully romantic resolution of the dilemma as he reached out to a religion of religions composed of 'the common elements in all religious affections' to be known by intuition. To be sure, Schleiermacher as a genuine Christian theologian, assigned a unique status, one of incomparable seniority it may be said, to Christianity, so much so he could declare: 'And so this comparison of Christianity with other religions is in itself sufficient warrant for saying that Christianity is, in fact, the most perfect of the most highly developed forms of religion (namely, the monotheistic ones).'[17] But it was sufficient for him to call Christianity the 'highest' religion; he did not ascribe absoluteness to it as he could not ascribe absoluteness to any 'positive' religion.

The problem of linking the idea of 'revelation' and 'revealed' to the idea of the 'positive' for the realm of historically actual religious communions[18] figures as a very large one for Schleiermacher, as he felt that if absoluteness or 'pure and entire truth' was claimed for any particular religious revelation such a claim would be contested by others.[19] On the contrary, he would argue that when it is realized that revelation is conditioned by 'the essence of human limitedness' – which, however, 'is not an infra-human ignorance concerning God' – then a scale could be set up according to which 'it may be truly said even of the imperfect forms of religion, so far as they can be traced, in whole or in part, to a particular starting-point and their content cannot be explained by anything previous to that point, that they rest upon revelation, however much error may be mingled in them with the truth'.[20] Not ony did he remove absoluteness from the concept of revelation but in true romantic fashion inclined at times to read revelation into nature itself. Thus by way of interpreting a Pauline statement, he would suggest that the world itself is 'the original revelation of God'.[21]

But something more than mere romantic inclination can also be perceived in Schleiermacher's view of revelation, namely a profound appreciation of transcendence, evidenced by such statements as the following, where he qualifies the view expressed above. 'No particular thing', says he, 'since it always belongs to the world can be regarded as divine revelation.'[22] So while we must leave the transcendent alone, we may still locate all revelations at various points in the scale of gradation, having regard also to the relativity of socio-cultural contexts in which they occur, or to use Schleiermacher's own words, 'the total state of the society'.[23] This last thought seems very important as it provides a viable scheme for accommodating the different bearers of revelation, 'the men who are credited with divine descent'.[24]

The thought of Hegel on this vital subject is very different. No doubt, as Kroner points out, 'he was a Romanticist in his longing for unity; he was anti-Romantic in the way he gratified his longing'.[25] The true Romantic would ignore differences as provincial but would adopt a policy of appeasement towards them while they are there. But Hegel had to seek a philosophical principle for genuinely reconciling them. Also, it should be noted, that like Schleiermacher and indeed like Fichte and Schelling, all of whom were under Kant's influence, Hegel too was much occupied with the problem of the relation between positive religion and revelation. Revelation for these other philosophers consisted in sheer inwardness, with which positive religion must be seen in sharp contrast. The Hegel of the *Early Theological Writings*, seems to have cheerily observed this distinction.[26] But the mature Hegel abandoned it in the light particularly of the theme developed in the *Logic*, which contended that the 'inward' and the 'outward' can be separated from each other only by mere abstraction. Hegel clarifies: 'The one is the abstraction of identity with self; the other of mere multiplicity or reality. But as stages of the one form they are essentially identical: so that whatever is put explicitly in one abstraction, is also as plainly and at one step only in the other. Therefore what is only internal is also external: and what is only external, is so far only at first internal.'[27] To take the essence to be merely internal, says Hegel, is 'the customary mistake of reflection'.[28]

In the light of Hegel's interpretation of the Spirit as dynamic, where contingency itself was assigned a place embraced in Reason, it was necessary to eschew all distinction between an ideal religion and historic religious realities even in their purely representational *(Vorstellung)* form. This completely harmonizes itself with his view that thought is not an activity of dealing with mere formal laws, divorced as it were from life and what is manifested in history and culture. It is his contention that one of the religions of history, Christianity, which is also 'the absolute religion' had already annihilated the distinction between ideal religion (which can exist only in a purely formal way) and the actual religions of history. But the path leading to that goal made it necessary for Hegel to distinguish between religion in general, consisting of the three moments of the Spirit, namely, *universality*, *particularity* and *individuality*, and definite religion composed of the many actual religions of the world both past and present.

Religion in general is, however, only an idea to be apprehended from the standpoint of the *subject* and it is necessary that it put itself forth into *objectivity*, and the way of doing so is to assume the form of the many definite religions. Hegel arranged all the known religions of the world according to a metaphysical scheme that reflects the unstable equilibrium, or even the state of separation, in which the three moments of the Spirit exist in them. (Obviously there is much for which to criticize Hegel in connection with this arrangement but the obligation to do so must be avoided in this treatise.)

Religion in general, Hegel tells us, became fully expressed in a 'positive religion',[29] which is distinct from all the definite religions of history. This positive religion is Christianity, which is also the absolute religion. There are several tests by which Hegel decided that Christianity is this religion, the main one being that it is both revealed and known as such.[30] It is the absolute religion because it is the complete self-expression of the idea *(Notion)* of religion known to us through religion in general.[31] Further, in view of Hegel's doctrine of 'the unity of identity and difference'[32] which the Spirit must accomplish, and of the absolutist speculative philosophy likewise, and also in view of another doctrine which says, 'the appearance shows nothing that is not in the essence and in the appearance there is nothing but what is manifested',[33] it is logical that actual historical religions be comprehended in the system.

Here we must pause to examine the specific scope Hegel gives to the method of comparison as the importance of doing so at this juncture has become evident. Some statements by Hegel seem to reflect a low esteem in which he held it. Thus, while conceding that it has led to some success 'in the provinces of comparative anatomy and comparative linguistics', he still cautions us: '[But] it is going too far to suppose that the comparative method can be employed with equal success in all branches of knowledge. Nor – and this must be emphasized – can mere comparison ever ultimately satisfy the requirements of science. Its results are indeed indispensable, but they are still labours only preliminary to truly intelligent cognition.'[34] However, close examination of the whole passage in which these words of caution occur will show that Hegel's criticism is directed towards what he styles 'external comparison', depending on 'immediate perception, i.e., Diversity or Variety' which ignores the fact that 'comparison has one and the same substratum for likeness and unlikeness'.[35] Likeness by itself is identity and unlikeness by itself is difference, but under the dynamic unity of the two both terms become dynamic and the substratum is recovered. What Hegel wants to make sure of is that in a proper act of comparison all external relations (involving a third thing) are internalized. So comparison becomes for Hegel an act within the Absolute and hence within the absolutist system.

Now, in so far as Christianity is the religious counterpart – as well as the basis – of that system it must comprehend other historical religions through speculative philosophy and what it does accomplish is simply to manifest in a true form the content which has already been there in essence and in principle. Commenting on Hegel's view, W. T. Stace observes:
'Christianity is the absolute religion because it has for its content absolute truth. Its content is, according to Hegel, identical with the Hegelian philosophy. Hegelianism is esoteric Christianity. For though the content is the same the form is different. Philosophy presents the absolute content in

the absolute form, the form of pure thought. Christianity presents this identical content in the form of the sensuous and pictorial thought, *Vorstellung*.'[36]

Stace's statement, while it is true enough, is so typical of a majority of Hegel scholars in that they do not perceive the reverse dependence of Hegel's philosophy as a whole upon Christianity. The following stipulation by Fackenheim seems to be a needed corrective:

'It is a central Hegelian doctrine that the true religion (Christianity) is the true 'content', lacking merely the true 'form' of speculative thought; that philosophy could not reach truth unless its true content pre-existed in religion; that philosophic thought therefore requires religion as its true basis in life, and that the true philosophy, in giving the true religious content its true form in thought, both transfigures religion and produces itself.'[37]

To advert a little to the main difference of Hegel's thought from Schleiermacher's on the subject, as outlined above, it can be briefly said to consist in, (1) the status of absoluteness ascribed to one religion, Christianity, and (2) the transformation of all religion, including Christianity, into the form of speculative philosophy by using comparative comprehension as a means to that end. It may also be said in brief that Hegel took religion far more seriously than Schleiermacher or any Romantic ever did or could. Religion was for him not one of the things philosophy dealt with; it was rather the whole foundation of philosophy. Of all the things that warranted thinking religion had the highest priority. In fact, it was religion that made philosophy necessary. Likewise, comparing the religions, for the sake of ultimate comprehension to be sure, was for him an incomparably more weighty matter than it was for Schleiermacher.

Hegel's contribution to comparative religion chiefly consisted in developing one approach (which he thought was the only possible one) to the philosophy underlying it. And this was by no means contemptible. His purpose was, far from producing a method of comparing religions in the technical sense, to show how speculative philosophy comprehends all religion – and every religion – by virtue of being grounded in one absolute religion which encompasses all, a fact, however, that cannot come to light except through its conscious re-enactment in the absolute (which is Hegel's) philosophy. Conversely, this philosophy also becomes what it is through the comprehension of religion. But philosophy is thought irreplaceable, for 'philosophic comprehension can *move through* non-Christian religions, when Christian faith, despite its comprehensive truth, can only confront them'.[38]

Hegel's great importance in the history of philosophy notwithstanding, his own approach to comparative religion was not further advanced by any of his followers and had no conspicuous representative in the later history of that discipline itself when it became a discipline, after Hegel's time. His approach, perhaps, could have been more important if his procedure had been reversed, that is to say, if speculative philosophy had been applied as *a means* for comparing the religions, as Hegel's philosophy was made use of for so many other kinds of investigations not excluding theology. Considering the reciprocal identity between 'reflection-into-self' and 'reflection-into-another',[39] so central a principle in Hegel's logic, this would have been natural. This seems to be the whole basis of his logic, which as a logic of life, that is to say, of Spirit, Reason, intuition and being, seeks life itself 'as the medium in which opposites both arise and dissolve'.[40] We must of course ignore something that intrudes itself into this context, namely, those unreflective, syncretistic theories of the unity of all religions, as they have no place in this consideration. As will become clear in the pages to follow, it will be our effort to set up modes of reflection-into-self and reflection-into-another, without trying to describe which is 'itself' and which is 'another'. However, the fact remains that Hegel's thought had not on the technical study of comparative religion anything remotely like the impact it had on social and political philosophy, philosophy of religion as such or theology, so much so the late Professor Jordan's statement to the effect that Hegel's relationship to comparative religion is 'slight and distant'[41] is entirely correct.

However, Hegel remains the only great philosopher who sought out the ways in which the Absolute expresses itself in and through the historical realities of actual religions, and in this respect he retains to this day a position unique among the philosophers. Immediately after Hegel's death, the story of German philosophy as Karl Löwith eminently makes clear,[42] was one of rejection of Hegel. But this rejection implied several things,[43] (1) a flight from Hegel, paradoxically accomplished, on the wings of the dialectics provided by Hegel,[44] a flight that included a return to Kant; (2) an 'exhaustion' of the spirit, with reference to idealism; (3) the coming to the fore of a number 'appendicies' to the history of philosophy which remained oblivious of 'the destructive force of the (Hegelian) movement', and (4) the degeneration of systematic religious (theological and philosophical) thought into 'history of dogma, church history, comparative religion, psychology of religion'. It is clearly indicated that comparative religion as a technical science arose as a result of the disintegration of Hegelian idealism, a consequence of the 'exhaustion' of the Spirit. But it must be recognized that what is mentioned here as comparative religion is the technical discipline in which form alone we know it. It is obvious that it could come only out of the break-up of idealism as it disregarded the very caution that Hegel had uttered with respect to the limitation of the comparative method.

In re-examining Hegel in this brief fashion we are not seeking a simple and straight road of return to Hegel but rather looking for new ways to fulfill, at least partially, an old, unfulfilled and albeit, only a slightly heard of, promise. But this promise must be taken out of the framework of Hegelian system, though not entirely, and certainly not out of philosophy, in order that it may see a new avenue of approach to fulfilment. We too live and think in the post-systematic era and we can accomplish our goal no more than in a fragmentary way, that is, by gathering such pieces as we can from the break-up of the great idealistic systems and by shaping them to suit our theoretical needs. Hence the 'spirit' has to be interpreted in other than absolutist terms, and not monistically at all, and in order to serve the purpose envisaged in this work, in the place of historical religions through which the spirit is supposed to explicate itself will have to be substituted the more nebulous but no less concrete actualities, knowable by existential traits of consciousness. And since the goal that is sought is a higher dimension of comparison as such rather than the Absolute that by definition must transcend all comparison, it will not be necessary to gather up or collect all such actualities. Also, collecting of all such actualities, if not empirically at least by providing a completely integrated deductive logical framework, within which all such actualities can be properly housed, is indeed essential in a system. On the contrary, given the nature of this essay, it will be necessary only to build up in an *eminent* way two such actualities into clearly distinct spheres so that the highest philosophical ends of comparison would be served, which is what we will undertake to do in the subsequent chapters.

Before we end this chapter on the philosophical scope of comparing in religion it will be just and fair to consider in brief a potentially powerful alternative, which originating in a different source and in a different tradition had unveiled a different programme of philosophically dealing with, though not of comprehending, all empirical actualities, including the religions. That alternative is pluralism or radical empiricism, a philosophy that was not only totally opposed to absolute idealism but had felt it necessary to denounce its fundamental tenets in order to set forth its own views. Undoubtedly, the greatest architect of this philosophy, particularly vis-à-vis the religions was William James, who wrote:

'[But] whereas absolutism thinks that [the said] substance becomes fully divine only in the form of totality and is not its real self in any form but the *all*-form, the pluralistic universe which I prefer to adopt is willing to believe that there may ultimately never be an all-form, that the substance of reality may never get totally collected, that some of it may remain outside of the largest contribution of it ever made, and that a distributive form of reality, the *each*-form, logically as acceptable and empirically as probable as the all-form commonly acquiesced in as so obviously the self-evident thing.'[45]

James himself applied his pluralistic view to the diverse phenomena of religion, particularly mysticism (his main object of interest) in his great classic, *Varieties of Religious Experience*. His conclusion is that the religious (particularly mystical) phenomena are 'too various' and 'too private' to be comprehended under a universal umbrella.[46]

Finally, it may be said that philosophy has kept moving as it had for hundreds of years and in the last hundred years comparative religion too has come a long way. But philosophy's interaction with comparative religion (either in the form of studying actual historical religions or in some more conceptualized form) has not come a long way. Rather a path unveiled by Hegel has remained not too well-trodden. In recent times, philosophy has developed largely along two lines, namely the philosophy of language and phenomenology. The former is probably more chained to its cultural origins than any other form of philosophy and is still unready to tackle problems beyond a limited language tradition and thought horizon. Phenomenology, on the contrary, has doubtless a greater ability to go into wider horizons and has the potentiality to acquire universal significance for the obvious reason that consciousness is more widespread in the world than any particular language. Here, however, we are more interested in the interaction of phenomenology as philosophy with comparative religion. In this respect, some advances have been made, and one would put Ernst Cassirer at the head of those who made them. There is obviously that branch of study called phenomenology of religion, a very important version of comparative religion. What are its limitations and what are its possibilities and in what further way can the involvement of philosophy be advanced? These are all some of the matters to which the rest of the book will be devoted, and therefore there is no warrant to engage in discussion of them just yet.

3

The Romantic Nursery of Comparative Religion and the Work of Max Müller

This chapter is meant to be a brief detour into the beginnings of comparative religion as a special discipline, involving as it did freedom from the previous dependence on philosophy. The science of religion ceased to be a 'science within philosophy' as Hegel had envisaged it.[1] The nature and scope of comparative religion as newly conceived is probably best expressed in the words of Louis Jordan who writes:

'Comparative Religion is that science which compares the origin, structure and characteristics of the various religions of the world, with a view to determining their genuine agreements and differences, the measure of relation in which they stand one to another and their relative superiority or inferiority when regarded as types. Otherwise expressed: Comparative Religion denotes the application and products of a particular method of research, – wherein, in the domain of Religion, one's ultimate conclusions are arrived at by a series of comparisons.'[2]

This definition covers a phase of the history of the discipline based on painstaking and scientific study, comprehending different fields of research, which began with a group of men of whom Friedrich Max Müller is generally thought to be the most famous modern pioneer. Max Müller, though not a philosopher himself was motivated by a deep philosophical impulse in his work. But his work had certain romantic antecedents that go back to the fathers of the Romantic Movement and hence to a time before Hegel; and at the earliest stages comparative religion had borne in it their unmistakable imprint.

The earliest relevant romanticist work to be noted is G. E. Lessing's *Die Erziehung des Menschengeschlechts* [The Education of the Human Race], first published in 1780. In the quest for the meaning of religion, Lessing seeks to bind education and revelation. That which education is to the individual, revelation is to the human race,' he writes. Further, 'Education gives to man nothing which he cannot educe out of himself; it gives him that which he might educe out of himself; only quicker and more easily. In the same way revelation gives nothing to the human species, which the human race left to itself might not attain; only it has given, and still gives to it, the most important of these things earlier.'[3]

At all odds, the most significant figure of the early Romantic Movement, as far as religion is concerned, is J. G. Herder. Herder advanced many thought-provoking ideas on myth and symbol and on nature itself. Nature, according to him, is reflected in human language, which is based on reproduction of sounds and images. The theme of education, of which nature is the medium, runs through Herder's writings, as it does through Lessing's. The medium of education is nature, 'the earliest document of the Human Race', which forms the title of his famous work on the subject, *Älteste Urkunde des Menschengeschlechts* (1774–6). He argues that nature itself is not a clear revelation but a symbolic hieroglyph, which needs to be deciphered.[4] This concern led him to study the nature-wisdom of ancient civilized people like the Egyptians, the Phoenicians and the Indians. Herder is known to be one of the real founders of the science of mythology, which through Schelling's more systematic inquiry resulted in the latter's *Philosophy of Mythology*. Herder felt that the languages of the nations must be used as keys to their mythologies as he conceived of an overarching unity that includes both these plus poetry. He believed that the comparative study of mythology is accompanied by the comparative study of language and that the two together would uncover the wisdom of nature which God has intended as the substance of man's education. Herder is the earliest among the moderns to grasp the relation between language and myth, which Walter Otto in our time, speaking with Herder's own accents, describes as inseparable and reciprocally related to the extent of being identical in fact (meaning that myth must be understood as language and language as myth).[5]

The romantic philosophy reached its high point where mythology, poetry and other non-rational expressions of the mind were clearly elevated to the highest level of thought, and both happened in Schelling. In his system of *Transcendental Idealism* as well as in his *Philosophy of Mythology* and *Philosophy of Revelation* was produced 'a synthesis of philosophy, history, myth, poetry such as had never appeared before'.[6] Having rejected all ideas of clear-cut distinction between 'the subjective and the objective', it turned to the belief in 'a spiritual universe' which forms 'a continuous, unbroken, organic whole'.[7]

Alongside of the romantic philosophers there was another group of romantic scholars, the symbolists. Among the latter the most famous are Joseph Von Görres and Friedrich Creuzer. Görres, who was mainly notable for the extravagant enthusiasm of his belief put forward in his *Mythengeschichte der Asiatische Welt* [The History of Myth in the Asiatic World], 1810, arguing that India was the primordial home of humanity. In that home, according to him, mankind lived in a paradisiacal state where there was perfect harmony with nature and with God. He believed that all traditions of the peoples of the world contain reminiscences of that state. This theme of the single origin of mankind was another inspiration that lay behind the quests of comparative philologists, particularly the pioneer of Indo-European philology, Franz Bopp, who established the theory that Sanskrit, Greek, Latin and the Germanic languages had all descended from one parent language.

Creuzer, Görres's contemporary and colleague, published the first part of *Symbolik und Mythologie der Alten Völker, besonders der Griechen* [Symbolism and Mythology of the Ancient peoples, especially the Greeks], also in 1810. Unlike Görres, Creuzer sought a more definite line of comparison between the Indians and the Greeks, the latter being the immediate parents of Western civilization. His tone was more restrained than Görres's. However, he sought to establish that oriental influences decisively determined the character of Homeric Greece. He tried confidently to establish through such comparative study the truth of the spiritual unity of all mankind. He used the principle of the symbol effectively to argue his theory, as symbol meant for him the direct revelation, rather than indirect mediation, of the gods.

This set the stage for the technical study of comparative religion. Whether Max Müller should be credited with the role of being the founder of the modern study of comparative religion or not is a small matter. In fact, there were others immediately before him who had made important beginnings. What cannot be denied, however, are the facts that he was the pioneer in organizing the discipline in the academic world by introducing it into the modern university, and that he was its most indefatigable public relations man. He was not a thinker of the stature of a Kant, a Hegel or a Schopenhauer, although without doubt he was one of the most generally educated men of the last century, a world-citizen with a great vision of human unity and potentiality. His great merit consists in the fact that he was able to focus attention on the worldwide phenomenon of religion by suitably orienting studies in philology, and to a lesser extent mythology, and that he was able to introduce into them the emphasis on the comparative method. Another aspect of his work that appeals to us is that he made his comparative study definitely and clearly one between Indian and European antiquities based on literary resources.

Max Müller tried to correct the one-sidedness of the study of mythology by the study of language, and he genuinely believed that the sources of the unity of mankind can be re-established by recovering, through the study of comparative philology, the original form of human consciousness. 'The earliest work of art, wrought by the human mind', he said, 'more ancient than any literary document, and prior even to the first whisperings of tradition – the human language forms an uninterrupted chain from the first dawn of history down to our own times.'[8] He saw comparative philology (as distinct from the science of language), whose origin he traces to Sir William Jones' founding of the Royal Asiatic Society in 1784,[9] and whose development through Schlegel, Bopp, Grimm, Burnouf and others, as a most vital discipline contributing to the comparative study of religion. He was convinced that comparative religion will not only indirectly benefit from comparative philology but can and must be directly modelled on it.

Through comparative philology we will arrive at an original form of consciousness, as he calls it the *primum cognitum*, which in each case expresses 'a general not an individual idea', and in each case acquires a corresponding *primum apellatum*.[10] 'Language', he observes, 'still bears the impress of the earliest thoughts of man, obliterated, it may be, buried under new thoughts, yet here and there still, recoverable in their sharp original outline'.[11] Therefore he believed that one must pursue language to its origins with the skill of an 'Indian trapper'.[12] This belief is truly accompanied by a romantic faith in the primitive man's advantages over the civilized man. So he writes: 'Man, in his primitive and perfect state, was not only endowed like the brute, with the power of expressing his sensations by interjections, and his perceptions by onomatopoeia. He possessed likewise the faculty of giving more articulate expression to the rational conceptions of his mind. That faculty was not of his own making. It was an instinct, an instinct of the mind as irresistible as any other instinct. So far as language is the production of that instinct, it belongs to the realm of nature.'[13]

Max Müller's philological theories which are certainly contested and repudiated by later philologists are not at issue here. What is solely of interest is how he sought to apply them to the study of the human phenomenon in question. Referring to the oldest of human words, he writes, 'They are all substantives, they express something substantial, something open to sensuous perception. Nor is it in the power of language to express originally anything except objects as nouns, and qualities as verbs. Hence the only definition we can give of language during that early state is, that it is the conscious expression in sound of impressions received by all the senses.'[14] This insight born of comparative philology, Max Müller argues, is absolutely necessary to correct the extravagent claims of the science of mythology. He argues the point that there is no such thing as mythological perception or consciousness independent of primary instincts, of which language was the means of expression and, paradoxically, was also the reason for its eventual self-alienation. Thus he writes, 'Man loses his instincts as he ceases to want them. His senses become fainter, when as in the case of scent, they become useless. Thus the creative faculty which gave to each conception, as it thrilled for the first time through the brain, a phonetic expression, became extinct when its object was fulfilled.'[15] Hence: 'Tedious as this may seem, we believe that while engaged in these considerations the mist of mythology will gradually clear away, and enable us to discover behind the floating clouds of the dawn of thought and language, that real nature which mythology has so long veiled and disguised.'[16] For instance, the discovery of the ancient names common in all Aryan languages, or 'the discovery that all these names had originally an expressive and poetical power' will alone explain the phenomenon of mythological language and 'render intelligible that phase of the human mind which gave birth to the extraordinary stories of gods and heroes – of gorgons and chimeras – of things that no human eye had ever seen, and no human mind in a healthy state could ever have conceived'.[17]

Max Müller's aim was to dethrone mythology from the exalted position in which it had been placed by Schelling, Creuzer, Görres and others. Mythology, he argues, is itself not an effective tool for the quest of the phenomena of man and his consciousness – and the primary product of that consciousness, namely, religion – as it is only 'a dialect of an ancient form of language'. 'Mythology', therefore, 'though chiefly concerned with nature and here again mostly with those manifestations which bear the character of law, order, power, and wisdom impressed on them, was applicable to all things. Nothing is excluded from mythological expression; neither morals nor philosophy, neither history nor religion, have escaped the spell of that ancient Sibyl. But mythology is neither philosophy, nor history, nor religion, nor ethics'.[18] It is in his view, a *quale* and not a *quid*. In this train of thought has been made one of the best known of Max Müller's statements: 'Mythology, which was the bane of the ancient world, is in truth a disease of language.'[19] This fact, he believes, is reflected in the process by which names of physically perceived objects were changed into names of gods and goddesses, as for instance, 'Hώς (dawn) became the wife of Tιθωνός, and *Fatum* (what had been spoken) the power called Fate. Agreeing with Ottfried Müller, he suggests: 'The mythic form of expression which changes all beings into persons, all relations into actions, is something so peculiar that we must admit for its growth a distinct period in the civilization of a people.'[20] Yet myth is not considered something that could have been avoided; it is only that myth must be understood as a form of language, and in order to know what myth really is it is necessary to explore language.

The problem of myth must be studied in the light of the relation between language and thought, as ever since Wilhelm von Humboldt it has been assumed that the two are inseparable. While Max Müller would accept this as a sound principle he would still add the amendment that language and thought are not the same thing.[21] Nevertheless, he admits that language necessarily reacts on thought as 'we see in this reaction, in this refraction of the rays of language, the real solution of the old riddle of mythology'.[22] 'Mythology', therefore, 'in the highest sense, is the power exercised by language on thought in every possible sphere of mental activity...'[23] The endeavours to construct philosophies of mythology in disregard of this fact meet with Max Müller's frowning disapproval; in fact he positively, and in very strong words, denounces Schelling's *Philosophy of Mythology*.[24] It is his firm opinion that mythology is incapable of being raised to philosophy; on the contrary, philosophy from Thales to Hegel has been 'an uninterrupted battle against mythology, a constant protest of thought against language'.[25] In respect of the Greeks, he says that most of their ancient myths in their literal meaning 'are absurd and irrational and frequently opposed to the principles of thought, religion, and morality which guided the Greeks as soon as they appear in the twilight of traditional history'.[26]

Now although he denies independence to mythology as a science, yet in the form of *comparative* mythology, that is, as a subsidiary of comparative philology – in his view the only valid general science of language – he sees in it an irreplaceable value for the task of wresting 'the original form and meaning of decayed words by the same means by which comparative grammar recovers the original form and meaning of terminations'.[27] 'My own work in Comparative Mythology', he declares, 'consisted chiefly in laying down some of the general principles of that science, and in the etymological interpretations of some of the ancient names of gods, goddesses and heroes'.[28] Max Müller makes comparative philology the mother discipline of comparative mythology and therefore also the primary tool for the study of comparative religion.

It seems that he strives to replace a hitherto prevailing unlimited faith in the science of myth with a similar faith in the science of language in the form of comparative philology in answering all questions relating to the primary phenomena of mankind and their origin. However, he has also produced a consistent theory comprehending all these matters. Comparative philology appears to him to be the basis of the other kinds of comparative studies, viz., in religion and mythology. At an appropriate place later on in this essay, we will question this assumption, as also some other assumptions, and will try to demonstrate why comparative phenomenology will alone be the truly comprehensive foundation for all kinds of comparative studies, whether in mythology, theology or language itself.

Now, despite the limitations of comparative philology in the sense that it is not the foolproof method that he thought it was, Max Müller himself, being one of the fathers of the comparative method in all human studies, has earned for himself an enduring place. Undoubtedly, he embraced such an approach with vigour and advocated it with fervour, and the content that he sought to put into it is by no means negligible. 'Why', he writes, 'all knowledge is acquired by comparison. It is said that the character of scientific research in our age is pre-eminently comparative, this really means that our researches are now based on the widest evidence that can be obtained, on the broadest inductions that can be obtained by the human mind.'[29] He literally adopted and sought to work out in his work Goethe's famous dictum:

'He who knows one language knows none.' Elsewhere, he writes, 'the *comparative spirit* is the truly scientific spirit of our age, nay of all ages. An empirical acquaintance with single facts does not constitute knowledge in the true sense of the word. All human knowledge begins with the two or the Dyad, the comprehension of two single things in one.'[30] What has been demonstrated as powerful and effective beyond dispute (as he would quote the testimony of such classical philologists as Mommsen and Curtius) he seeks to apply to the study of religion also.

Max Müller considers comparative philology as both a tool and a model for research in religion. Language and religion are two phenomena that have the closest similarity with each other, both originating in the instinctual life of man and exhibiting a remarkable continuity of development. His theory of the origin and development of religion built on the model of language and worked out in several of his lectures and essays, most notably in his definitive work, *Lectures on the Origin and Growth of Religion*,[31] must be seen in the context of his view of the essential affinity between these two. 'Of religion, too', he observes, 'as of language, it may be said that in it everything new is old and everything old is new, and that there has been no entirely new religion since the beginning of the world'.[32] Like language, religion has been there from the beginning of history and its development is nothing but 'a succession of the new combination of the same radical elements'.[33] However, on occasions he doubted 'whether the time has yet come for attempting to trace, after the model of the Science of Language, the definite outlines of the Science of Religion'.[34] But he was cheered and encouraged by the then recent recovery of the canonical texts of the Vedas, the Avesta and the Tripiṭaka as well as the discovery of the real origin of the Greek, Roman and the European mythologies, not to speak of the already vast corpus of material on the Semitic religions.

As language is the tool and the model for the study of religion it was quite natural for him to argue: 'A patient study of the Sacred Scriptures of the world is what is wanted at present, more than anything else, in order to clear our own ideas of the origin, nature and purposes of religion.'[35]

The notable points in Max Müller's method as already evident are the following: (1) the case of comparative philology as both a tool and as a model for the study of comparative religion; (2) the stress on comparison as such; (3) the dependence on the sacred texts of the great religions; (4) the quest for origins and the definition of religion. The last point itself which has been so much a preoccupation in most inquiries in religion has been delibe- rately excluded from independent consideration here. The first two points have been discussed in some detail already; hence we will turn briefly to the third.

On the whole the bulk of Max Müller's work was concentrated on the comparison between the European and the Indian worlds, a circumscription which the present author also accepts, but with an emphasis altogether different. Max Müller, as already explained, is essentially a romantic, and he looked upon India with that predilection, which comes through frequently, as when he triumphantly declares: 'the East, formerly a land of dreams, of fables and fairies, has become to us a land of unmistakable reality; the curtain between the East and the West has been lifted, and our old forgotten home stands before us again in bright colours and definite outlines. Two worlds separated for thousands of years, have been reunited as by a magic spell...'[36] It cannot be gainsaid that the philosophical goal of his work in comparative religion, mythology and philology was precisely to make an epistemic reunion possible and effective by recalling the memories of a common antiquity that stretches even beyond the dim light of early history. Perhaps he may have gone farther than he intended in announcing that the East is the foundation of all Western civilization. [37]In unearthing 'the petri- fied language of ancient India and Greece' the practical purpose was to establish that the word of God has been revealed 'where alone it can be revealed – revealed in the heart of man', and to disclose 'the image of the Father, the Father of all the nations upon earth'.[38] Max Müller's longing for unity at both the epistemic and practical levels, therefore, was truly romantic. Even Hegel, as Kroner points out, was a romantic in this longing for unity, but 'he was anti-romantic in the way he carried out this longing'.[39] For Hegel this unity was to be achieved by the Spirit *(Geist)* and the dialectics of history and the 'laws of thought' are simply expressive of what the Spirit is striving. Boundaries are there not to be simply ignored but to be overcome by the Spirit, and Life itself cannot fully reflect the work of the Spirit.[40] For Max Müller, it is all a simple romantic alternative, of picking one's way to the origins through comparative studies and reaching out to a com- mon antiquity before their erection.

A final evaluation of Max Müller's pioneer work in comparative religion – and along with it comparative studies in some allied fields also – as has been discussed, is in place. The unity of his ideas and his principal objectives and methods have all been briefly treated already. Every science grows by revising and often rejecting the ideas of its originator or originators. Here Max Müller's fate within the history of the comparative study of religion is not exceptional. More than any specific scientific contribution he has made – he has made many, and most are controversial – his place in the last analysis must be estimated in terms of the role he played as a statesman and an outstanding promoter, in the years of its inception, of this new discipline. But for him, comparative religion, history of religion, phenomenology of religion, *Religionswissenschaft*, or whatever else it is called, as distinguished from theology, would not have found a place in the modern university. Besides, he forced the issue of juxtaposing in some fashion, the spiritual histories of the East along with that of Europe in serious academic inquiries. So he writes:

'Before all a study of the East has taught us the same lesson which the Northern nations once learnt in Rome and Athens, that there are other worlds besides our own, that there are other religions, other mythologies, other laws, and that the history of philosophy from Thales to Hegel is not the history of human thought. In all these subjects the East has supplied us with parallels, and with all that is implied in parallels, viz., the possibility of comparing, measuring and understanding.'[41]

Having given this estimate of Max Müller's work, the lines of departure that we take from his thought, as have already been indicated and will be shown more fully in this essay, may be expressed thus: (1) comparative philology will be replaced by comparative phenomenology, to conceive it being the major objective of this inquiry, which naturally will assume the position of the mother discipline, comprehending mythology, theology, ontology, and philology itself; (2) the goal of unity, while in nowise rejected, will appear to become indefinitely postponed, the need to see deeply into diversity being maintained. No programme of unity, epistemic or practical, it will be implied, can deliver what it promises, as the clear need is to look at the very centres of the different spiritual spheres.

4

Comparative Religion as History of Religions and the Quest for Historical Self-knowledge

Very soon after the time of Max Müller comparative religion began to develop as an enormously ramified and diversified field of study. It was often modelled on, and also fed by, other disciplines, thus terminating an era of excessive dependence upon the romantic versions of mythology and philology, which themselves incidentally acquired new dimensions. These other disciplines are history, anthropology, ethnology, psychology, sociology, and linguistics. During the last decades many books of all kinds have been poured into the market, and today especially a large variety of books, both original and unoriginal, are being produced as comparative religion has become a popular subject in the list of human studies.

The comparative method is common to all these sciences, having been assisted by them in turn in its development. It is quite true that in modern times it is the life sciences, viz., botany, biology and physiology, that have helped to recover the comparative method as it had suffered oblivion under the reign of the abstract natural sciences with their dominant interest in discovering universal laws and homogeneous elements resulting inevitably in losing sight of the factor of individuality. Undoubtedly, it was that particular line of scientific development beginning with Linnaeus and culminating with Darwin that paved the way for the return of the individuality principle in natural species through the method of comparison. But this fact, as Dilthey, a writer whom we will soon consider here, points out, spelt both advantages and disadvantages to the human sciences in that they tended to use the life sciences as perfect models and to uncritically transfer the concepts as well as the entire apparatus of comparative method from them.[1]

No doubt, the comparative method itself is well established in all forms of modern scientific inquiry and has been amply in evidence in the human sciences like anthropology, sociology and history, on which comparative religion has depended for so long for nurture. This means that the validity of the method itself is no longer in question. But a certain problem has had to be resolved, namely, how the method is used in the fields of human studies generally, including religion. This is a problem that has occupied some very able minds since the final decades of the last century, at the head of whose list must be placed Rickert, Windelband, Dilthey and Collingwood, the last named two above all. Dilthey's own ideas pertaining to the limits of objectivity in the human sciences dealing as they do with what he calls 'dynamic systems' were truly definitive.[2] Credit must be given to these men and a host of others for setting up the terms for the study of the human sciences and releasing them to a considerable extent from bondage to the methods of the natural sciences. This quest is among the various philosophical forces that have made possible some revolutionary approaches to the study of these, eventually to be brought under the rubric of 'phenomenology'.

In this connection one particular discipline which has had a very powerful impact upon philosophy, namely the philosophy of history, must be mentioned and considered in brief. An additional reason for considering it is that one of the widely accepted and influential alternative paths in the study of religion is the discipline of the history of religions. In the hands of men like Dilthey and Collingwood history became the ideal human science. Dilthey himself, after laying the groundwork for his great treatise envisaged as *Einleitung in die Geisteswissenschaften*, according to a very comprehensive scheme, is reported to have ultimately changed his direction to the *Kritik der historischen Vernunft*, which whether so intended or not, really represent his method as a whole. While he acknowledges his debt to the transcendental philosophy, and to Kant and Fichte in particular, as well as to Hegel, he advanced his own belief, expressed systematically already in his previous works, the *Einleitung* and *Abhandlungen zur Grundlegung der Geisteswissenschaften*, that the total human nature is the basis of epistemology. Here Dilthey speaks actually as an anti-rationalist. 'Thought is not', he writes, 'the source of form and meaning in experience; it merely elicits the form and meaning which are there already, and by following up beyond lived experience, the relations which are found in lived experience, pursues its endless task of exploiting the world-order.'[3] The gist of his view of history is clearly expressed as follows: 'From the basic function of understanding upward, lived experience, experience relived, and universal truths are bound together. The formation of concepts is not based on norms or values appearing beyond the world of objective knowledge, but arises from the tendency, dominant in all conceptual thought, to show up what is firm and enduring in the flow of events.'[4]

It is in this setting that we must re-examine that particular tradition of religious study called the history of religions. Undoubtedly, as we will perceive, the early historians of religions were for the most part philosophically naive and had adopted methods not educated by any profound philosophy of history. This tradition is still a lively one and has even today many representatives who exhibit varying degrees of philosophical sophistication. In a genuine sense the Dutch scholar, Cornelius Tiele may be regarded as its founder. In his *Gifford Lectures* at Edinburgh, he observed, 'I have been engaged in historical inquiries more than anything else, and all the more considerable works I have published have been of a historical kind. My late friend Kuenen used to say, "I am nothing if not critical!" I would venture to say of myself, "I am nothing if not historical".'[5] Along with Tiele, among the pioneers of this tradition, must be counted the Dutch scholar, Pierre Daniel Chantepie de la Saussaye

Undoubtedly, the history of religions was, in its early stages, not influenced, much less controlled, by any profound understanding of history as such. It is in this respect that philosophies of history such as enunciated by Dilthey will have to appear with their cardinal function in reshaping the whole method of the history of religions. Through the instrumentality of a philosophy of history, history of religions itself will have to be rendered into a science fruitful for philosophy. In this connection it will be remembered that Hegel's idealistic *Philosophy of History* (or for that matter his *Philosophy of Religion*) was not only not appropriated but rejected by historians of religions, one should add, due to profound misunderstanding. However, a reason – not what motivated the historians – for rejecting Hegel's view of history, is that his presentation of history as the all-comprehending realm of Reality would raise serious qualms in many minds. But under the aegis of the thought of men like Dilthey, the relation between the philosophical understanding of history and the historical understanding of religion could be re-opened as an important issue.[6]

However, Dilthey's starting-point may be called into question, as he regards religion as one of the products of the mind, living traditions to be listed along with art, philosophy, family, civil society, law and the state, and believes that 'it is just in their mighty forms that the mind of man objectifies itself and is known in them'.[7] On the other hand, in comparative religion proper in its genuine philosophical expression, it is legitimate to treat religion as the pre-eminent avenue for whatever knowledge is held to be the uniform objective of these above-mentioned expressions of historical reality. The method it adopts must suit the subject-matter and must automatically reveal the intrinsic character of religion as distinct from all other phenomena or expressions of Reality. What then is the uniform but implicit objective of all human sciences to which religion is the pre-eminent path? It is basically this: a form of knowledge to be defined as none other than self-knowledge, although besides it, religion by its very nature has surely other equally intrinsic goals, salvation (or *mukti, nirvāna*) above all, and knowledge of God or Reality in most cases. In the common denomination of self-knowledge all human sciences coincide, and it is well known that through the revolution effected by phenomenology those social sicences that had been, to begin with, modelled on the natural sciences have been able to come to grips, implicitly or explicitly, with the same problem of self-knowledge.

The history of religions then must be re-constituted in the light of profound interpretations of the philosophy of history, with an eye to self-knowledge in the realm of history. Although some historians of religion in recent decades have attempted to re-orient their discipline precisely in the light of profound philosophies of history, the clarity as to the objective to be realized, namely historical self-knowledge, has not been fully achieved. The history of religions as an exercise in the comparative study of religion is yet far from having gained a clear vision of the theoretical goal of its enterprise. All too often the question pertaining to the goal is tacitly answered by advancing a definition of religion or by giving an account of the origin of religion, each of which in its own way is an unfortunate fixation that has inhibited and hindered genuine progress in the philosophical dimensions of the discipline.

The following fact must never be forgotten. Every particular religion dissolves within its essence, by which is meant that it gives no thought to, such questions as 'What is religion?' and 'How did religion originate?'. As these questions do not cater to any existential, inner-structural demand of any known religion, they must, from the inside point of view of each, be deemed superfluous. As there is no category called 'religion' within the religions, the conclusion must be arrived at that there is no singular historical entitly answering to the word. Religions themselves ask their questions as conditioned by certain authoritative beliefs, perceptions and cognitions presented in their 'revelations' which from the outside *may be* seen as purely mythic. These are questions about God (or the gods), world, man, human destiny, Being (or beings), salvation, etc., but never about religion. So the only way to apprehend religion is to apprehend the religions as they ask their questions or follow the corresponding pursuits germaine to them and also *significantly* fail to do what is not theirs.

Therefore, the historical understanding of the religions must be true to the struggle of the religions themselves, which will be the measure of the self-knowledge to be sought in the realm of history, whose core, however, must have been defined *a priori* in terms of that struggle. This is the way in which the history of religions can become the source of a specific form of historical self-knowledge. But by defining the problem thus, one has already passed from the confines of history, wrongly conceived as the totality of reality, to the wider realms of phenomena; and self-knowledge likewise has been transferred to the broader foundations of phenomenology. Thus inevitably, historical self-knowledge must seek completion in phenomenological self-knowledge. There should remain no more valid grounds for interest in defining religion or accounting for its genesis, as has been done, favourably all the way from Plato to Schleiermacher and Paul Tillich, and desparagingly from Xenophanes to Feuerbach, Freud and Bertrand Russell.

Interest must shift to the phenomena of religion themselves as somehow integral to human consciousness, without asking extraneous questions, however important, about their truthfulness or veracity. It is enough for phenomenological self-knowledge to be true to the phenomena. But to confine oneself to the fine line of phenomenological self-knowledge without straying into the ultimate ontological truth questions of religious beliefs, offers a difficulty of the first magnitude, intellectually more than anything else. It indeed calls for the skill of one who walks the narrow ridge backed up by a strong resolution. Feuerbach may be cited as a notable case in point to demonstrate the riskiness of the enterprise. His view voiced condemningly indeed, cannot be truer, no doubt. He wrote: 'Historical expositions of various religions and mythologies of the peoples of the earth *without a true insight into religion* are to be found.'[8] And he was absolutely right in viewing the end of the study of religion as the gaining of self-knowledge by man, although unfortunately, he could only conceive it negatively, as he declared, 'I negate the fantastic hypocrisy of theology and religion only in order to affirm the true nature of man.'[9] He felt justified, nevertheless, as 'every negation in the realm of science is a positive act of the mind.'[10] But he could not, perhaps by virtue of the very nature of his presuppositions, withhold himself from going overboard into ontological truth questions and consequently made self-knowledge rather inversely ontological. Thus he proclaimed: 'True, it follows from my doctrine that there is no God, no abstract disembodied being distinct from nature and man who decides the fate of the world and of mankind as He pleases; but this negation is merely a consequence of an insight into the essence of God, of the knowledge that denotes nothing other than on the one hand the essence of nature and, on the other, the essence of man.'[11] It is absolutely necessary that phenomenology must recognize two kinds of self-knowledge, assigned to two levels of being, no matter whether conceived in the form of one's own self or otherwise, the one phenomenal and the other beyond it and no matter also whether sometimes conceived negatively as non-being. The phenomenal level is its own while that which is beyond is not. But in an activity such as the phenomenological study of religion where the phenomenon is religion itself, the integral and inherent place given to knowledge of the beyond, which is what makes it unique and distinct from all other phenomena, must be taken fully into consideration. Thus self-knowledge obtained by the phenomenological method is always inconclusive as it pertains to, and subserves, a level of knowledge that is transcendent by definition, However, why the religions are thus and not otherwise, that is to say, why they concern transcendental self-knowledge – either as demand only or as actuality – is more than a definitional issue for phenomenology, Socrates, the paradigmatic seeker of self-knowledge, indicates this as we are told in the *Φαεδρυς* that refusing to be drawn into a discussion of the myth concerning *Βορεας* carrying away *'Ωρείθυια* – and myths concerning the gods in general – he stubbornly stuck to the Delphic command *γνῶθι σεαυτόν* [know thyself].[12] The eternal starting-point of philosophy is neither the actualizability nor the non-actualizability of transcendent self-knowledge but the paradox that, while the self is unable to know itself, every form of knowledge hinges on its being, contrariwise, able to do so. Obviously, thorough-going positivism, which rejects such a paradox along with the whole dialectic of self-knowledge considers itself exempt; but then the recovery of positivism, if perchance that were to be attempted at all, may have to begin by the patient method of phenomenologically relocating it in one of the many mansions of the house of scepticism, which in the last resort has reference to the problem of self-knowing.

Transcendent self-knowledge and revelation constitute the two Archimedean points in religion's own epistemology. Undoubtedly, even Buddhism as religion – which it is – is based on these two, a matter that can be convincingly demonstrated by a correct study of the sources of authoritative knowledge in the Buddhist texts. Controversies as to the relative status of these two in official theological discussions have no reason to be imported here.[13] But it can be said in brief that the relation between them has been expressed in one of three ways, which are: (1) Starting from revelation as the Archimedean point, self-knowledge is so placed as to appear a mere corollary to it – often in some extremely dogmatic theological formulations as in Karl Barth's as a mere existential corollary.[14] (2) Starting from the opposite direction, revelation is placed within the dialectics of self-knowledge as one of its terms, as is predominantly the case with forms of philosophy of religion that have a Platonic foundation. (3) The two Archimedian points are identified as one and the same, most remarkably and classically expressed in the Upaniṣads. That the Upaniṣads present the most perfectly consistent and by far the most thoroughly developed doctrines of the self and self-knowledge is indisputable. (Buddhism must be understood as representing the obverse side of these doctrines, and in the last resort as making them more meaningful by challenging them to their ultimate foundations and hence radicalizing them). And a goodly portion of these famous sacred texts are about these. Because of its wholly transcendent character, knowledge of the self can be appropriated, it is argued by Yājnavalkya, the greatest of its spokesmen, only negatively as *neti, neti* [not this, not this].[15] The highest expression of this line of thought is found in the greatest Upaniṣadic text of all which says *Tat tvam asi* [That art Thou].[16] But such knowledge, it is also said elsewhere, does not come except through revelation, as stated in the *Kaṭha Upaniṣad* (I.2.23): 'This self cannot be attained by instruction nor by intellectual power, nor even through much hearing. He is to be attained only by the one whom he (the self) chooses. To such a one the self reveals its own nature.'[17]

As the epistemological goal of comparative religious study is different from the religions, so the sources of its knowledge are likewise different. Its sources of knowledge are only the religions as they are controlled and conditioned by these two Archimedean points and not the Archimedean points themselves as it is the case with the religions. Clearly then, the metaphysical issues that are alive in the religions with regard to both their sources of knowledge and their goal are not present in comparative religion, approached phenomenologically. Obversely, as the phenomenon of religion is elliptically linked to an altogether unique human activity which proceeds from the special sources and strains towards the special goals as indicated, it cannot be understood unless one studies it in strict conformity to these facts.

The two Archimedian points in the epistemology of religion, surely, do not exhaust the contents of religion that phenomenology must seek to understand, as it also concerns such central objectives of religion as salvation (or *mukti, nirvāṇa*). Hence the phenomenological self-knowledge is not a direct derivative of the transcendent knowledge implicit in the religion. There are other elements to be considered. The reasons for studying religion to the end that man may know himself, are obvious.

For of all human phenomena the one that should be regarded unquestionably as the outgrowth of man's engagement with his own existence, in a problematic manner, is what is known as religion. This being so, the essence of religion depends on, and cannot be concretized any more than, the essence of man himself. The impossiblity of concretizing both of these appear together as one, which too is mediated, in no other way than in the form of religion. Existence is not essence concretized, as the difference between the two is categorical. The problem of religion would become vastly complicated if it were to be discretely separated from the problem of man because it has neither essence nor existence nor any kind of being whatsoever apart from man. Nevertheless, the fact remains that no phenomenon of man is so internal and so integral to him as religion. Further, like man, it is thoroughly unobjectifiable in spite of all 'objective' representations, rites and manifestations which usually – and wrongly – constitute the subject-matter of comparative studies in religion.

This brief discussion here in this chapter, it is hoped, will have made some contributions towards clarifying what the real goal of the discipline of comparative religion ought to be. It has been argued that it is to gain a dimension of self-knowledge pertaining to a peculiar, human – and peculiarly human – activity called by the name of religion. The ontological and transcendent aspects of this activity except as they impinge upon and govern this activity itself, it has been resolved, overtly fall outside the range of this quest, although it has to be borne in mind that a hidden but deep interest in them must remain always suspended in the background. For, if religion ceases to be religion by reason of definition or neglect of definition, then there should remain nothing in it to be studied even phenomenologically. The fact that we study it at all presupposes not only that it is something, which goes without saying, but that it also *indicates* something, suggesting a comprehensible truth. Phenomenology should be content for the time being – and it is always in the time of the time being – to perceive that this truth is about man himself, without, however, ever wanting to shut off the possibility that it might also be about something above and beyond man, if only to avoid definitional self-contradiction. In this way all ontological statements can be transposed to the dialectical scheme of self-knowledge. Thus, for instance, when we say something about God, including his existence, we are saying something about man in an eminent manner that cannot be said in any other way. Seen from the angle of ontology this is the minimum truth, what it is *at least*. But from the point of view of phenomenology the *at least* must necessarily and deliberately become the *at most*, as it must stubbornly refuse to accommodate anything else *within* its framework. But the dialectic between the *at least* and the *at most* must continue to abide. Therefore, in principle, phenomenology will have no reason to be partial towards theistic positions as against atheistic ones, or towards idealist positions as against radically materialist ones, as they perform complementary functions in the dialectic of self-knowing; from its standpoint ontological affirmations and negations are not distinguishable in status and they do not affect the human reality of religion. This last does not, however, mean that these oppositions should be ignored, (or that propositionally they should be regarded as bearing equal truth) but that, on the contrary, they should be taken with the utmost seriousness as they do inform the self about itself, concerning some dimensions of its being, in a way that nothing else can. The same power vested in man and the same anguish come into play when he affirms God's existence as when he denies it. Through the affirmation or denial of Divine *existence* what is immediately revealed is something of the human *essence*. But this has to be said without implying: (1) reduction of ontological questions to phenomenological ones; (2) rejection of such questions; (3) attempt at direct resolution of them. The only path open, therefore, is bracketing them, that is to say, bracketing them *in*, rather than *out*. This path makes it possible for the religions themselves to resolve them and phenomenology's task would be to watch and understand them as they do so.

It has been instituted that the real but all too often unmanifest purpose in comparing the religions is the gaining of self-knowledge on man's part by pondering on an activity that is truly and characteristically human. This then brings us to a juncture at which we must move forward to examine some phenomenological theories of religion, a task to which we shall turn presently. But in considering these, our purpose would be to show that even the efforts to understand religion as something that appears – true to the spirit of descriptive phenomenology – will not make sufficient sense unless such understanding becomes a means to self-knowledge, which is the primary and we should add *transcendental*, obligation of man towards himself and towards all, in other words his highest epistemological imperative, as it will be the firm foundation for anything else worth the name of knowledge.

5

Some Phenomenological Theories of Religion

The term 'phenomenology of religion' is so widely used – and misused – today that it is difficult to say what it really applies to or what is common among all those theories which refer to themselves by that name. It is also difficult to tell who are properly to be called phenomenologists of religion. Some writers seem to intensify the confusion as they incline to take the history of phenomenological research further and further back in time, as does, for instance, G. van der Leeuw,[1] a notable phenomenologist of religion himself, who considers Chantepie de la Saussaye to represent an important landmark in it and again, in the same context, describes an earlier writer in comparative religion, Christoph Meiners (1747–1810) of Göttingen to be the first systematic writer who studied religion phenomenologically, and even refers to Benjamin Constant (1767–1830), a Frenchman in the same vein. There is no knowing where this process will end.

It is necessary, therefore, to say in some simple terms what the phenomenological procedure in religious study is, stopping short, indeed, of advancing a definition, for the mere sake at least of avoiding arbitrariness in enumerating writers as phenomenologists. Put simply and clearly, the phenomenological approach to religion means on the one hand, the seeking and the finding of some element in human consciousness where religion may be demonstrated to repose terminally and finally as far as we can see, and on the other, establishing the relations between religion thus located and its appearing to man and in civilization as a phenomenon. This is the only thing that ought to be axiomatic in phenomenology of religion and a great deal of confusion can be avoided if one adheres to this description faithfully. And once this is accepted a great many variations will be seen as possible. The truly revolutionary aspect of the phenomenological investigation of religion is that through it there has implicitly taken place a shift from all other realms of reality to the realm of consciousness as the primary focal point in the quest for religion's essence.

Obviously, because of the stress on consciousness one might suspect a profound affinity between phenomenology of religion and certain forms of psychology, as exemplified indeed by a number of eminent scholars.[2] But on closer examination affinity will be seen to give way to deep divergence. Accordingly, it will become clear that phenomenology of religion: (1) will seek neither to explain away nor even to explain religion but only to illuminate it in terms of the dynamics of consciousness; (2) will want to retain an ultimate sense of mystery in respect of consciousness and religion often by cherishing a sense of the holy or the sacred; (3) will rather seek to incorporate the appearance of the incomprehensible as it is as a necessary element in human self-comprehension; (4) will not rule out the question of the transcendent *per se* but will be committed to accommodating it, either in its negative or positive disposition, in that immense gap perpetually present at the heart of man's knowledge of Reality.

Another matter of the greatest importance in phenomenology is that consciousness itself has to be perceived and examined as a phenomenon; it is vitally necessary indeed when we look for the essence of religion in consciousness. Accordingly, the subjective must be apprehended objectively, the individual in the form of the general, for undoubtedly, phenomenology as science is possible only this wise. The expressions of religious consciousness can therefore be studied just as other phenomena, even phenomena of nature, are studied, but with a difference in so far as they reveal something that is most deeply subjective. Poetry and ritual are indeed similar to them and are invariably their vehicles. Not only the expressions but one's participation in the ultimate forms of religious – or for that matter all profoundly existential – forms of awareness is possible only through the channels of the symbolic. By symbol one does not mean some deliberate contrivance – although in an artistic sense it is that too – but every kind of awareness by which one comes to a knowledge of that which exceeds and surpasses one's own innate experience, in other words, an inherent and spontaneous defiance of the limits of experience, whether directed towards transcendent objects or simply generalized other objects of intrinsic significance.[3] Thus those objects of knowledge like sin (even one's own sinfulness) and anxiety and, contrariwise, salvational felicity and tranquillity become more clearly known to us through the channels of the symbolic, by coming into contact with the knowledge funded in society and civilization. Often they remain lively only to the extent to which such contact is vitally maintained. It has been seen that every serious phenomenologist of religion takes a deep interest in the symbol, though differences in interpretation prevail. But most phenomenologists also err in that, in their concern to advance a theory of the symbol, they seem to make it subserve some ontological end or some specifically mystical end. That practice has much to be said against it. But we must postpone criticism of it for approximate contexts that will offer themselves later in this essay.

However, when we look deeply into consciousness and religion through the symbolic we will see that our self-knowledge too, and inescapably, is symbolic in character. We do not see ourselves truly; we do not perceive the depth and the height of our being. Nor can we really know the terror of loneliness, suffering, anxiety, mortality, etc., except at their shallow levels, that is, except where they coincide with the limits of human capacity to feel, to be aware, conditioned by innate lethargy, sloth, unawakefulness, as well as by hope, desire, will and worldly love. In other words, where they coincide with life and its longings they are already terminated, and henceforth are mediated to us through the symbolic forms made possible by society and civilization. Only the god-men, those revealers, those paradigmatic persons, the pillars upon which historical religions rest, were, at least in principle, able to have known the heights and the depths of these things in reality, without the mediation of symbols. The phenomenologist of religion must deepen and enlarge human self-knowledge not indeed by negating the symbolic in religion but by reflecting the more deeply upon it, in all its variety and even apparent oppositions.

Now we must consider a few phenomenologists of religion, but using inherent quality and widespread influence as norms of judgment we will be justified in limiting the list here to just three outstanding modern writers in comparative religion, Rudolf Otto, G. van der Leeuw and Mircea Eliade. Besides, each one of these men has a distinct approach to the elucidating of the problem of religion and the field of comparative religion in terms of the criterion of phenomenology of religion that we have enunciated.

RUDOLF OTTO

Otto studied the religious phenomena directly in the context of Kantian philosophy rather than of what has come to be called phenomenology in recent times. To be specifically noted is Kant's well-known insistence on the one hand of the unknowability of the thing-in-itself, and, on the other, on the value of reflection. With regard to the latter, Kant had written:

'Reflection *(reflexio)* does not concern itself with objects themselves with a view to deriving concepts from them directly, but is that state of mind in which we first set ourselves to discover the subjective conditions under which (alone) we are able to arrive at concepts. It is the consciousness of the relation of given representations to our different sources of knowledge; and only by way of such consciousness can the relation of the sources of knowledge to one another be rightly determined.'[4]

Otto proceeds from such an act of reflection and then links it with the question of the thing-in-itself. Thus he gave wide currency in a specifically religious parlance to two words, *numen*, standing for Reality, and *numinous*, derived from the former. Otto has intended this theory to be an answer to Kant's agnosticism but essentially within Kant's own epistemological framework. He introduces his method thus: 'I shall speak of a unique "numinous" category of value and of a definitely "numinous" state of mind, which is always found wherever the category is applied.'[5] This state of mind is stated to be *sui generis*.[6] Otto's theory is that reason and its limit likewise being set aside, Reality manifests itself in consciousness by means of a peculiar means of apprehension called by the name of the numinous sense. Yet the emphasis in his theory, as Rickert somewhere points out, is not on the psychological process indicated by the term 'numinous sense' but on the Holy as such which is completely objective.

Hence, Otto's phenomenology is not confined to a psychological study of consciousness. Rather it is concerned primarily with the object manifested through its peculiar constitution. This object is referred to as 'the numinous'.[7] It is stated unequivocally that 'the numinous is objective and outside the self'.[8] Otto is careful to make sure that his analysis of the numinous sense *(das numinose Gefühl)* as a primary datum of consciousness does not lead one to the error of subjectivism. It must never be forgotten that his over-riding concern is with how the Supreme Reality reveals itself to man. Accordingly, he rejected Schleiermacher's theory of 'the feeling of dependence' as an inadequate account of religious consciousness. Otto, however, did not question the existence of such a feeling but thought it to be 'primarily a sort of self-consciousness, a feeling concerning oneself in a special, determined relation, viz., one's dependence', and feared that in its light one can come upon the fact of God only as the result of an inference.[9] Otto was convinced that 'holiness – the holy – is a category of interpretation and valuation peculiar to the sphere of religion'[10], but also that it could also be found in the wider domains of life. What was hoped to be achieved by his studies in comparative religion, as methodically outlined in his masterpiece, *Das Heilige* [The Idea of the Holy] was to provide a viable alternative to the illusion of rationality under which theology and comparative religion had so long laboured – a fact which, Otto has noted, had been perceived with a keener insight by the enemies of religion than by its champions and academic protagonists. This represents Otto's essential epistemological objective, consistently elaborated in several of his works. His theory is the best we have of an empirically grounded and philosophically articulated analysis of the non-rational in religion. It simply has not been bettered anywhere nor even equalled.

The greatness of Otto's contribution to the phenomenology of religion must doubtless be recognized. Nevertheless, a few queries can be addressed to his magnificent theory. While it is a most challenging philosophical depiction of mystical awareness, the effort to reconstruct the whole of religion from such heights must raise some doubts. The use of a special form of consciousness, the numinous sense, as the foundation for a general theory of religion does contain some weaknesses. By contrast, Schleiermacher's theory, despite its defects in other respects, seems to be more phenomenologically grounded, as the feeling of dependence is a universal and constant character of human consciousness, corroborated also by subjective reflection, than a theory such as Otto's based on verified incidences of a highly specialized form of awareness. Dependence on an element in consciousness that is extraordinary, actually and by definition, indeed reflects some limitations in the theory, which for that reason cannot be easily fitted into the phenomenological mould. Further the employment of a special phenomenological analysis for an ontological purpose, that is to say, to prove the existence of a self-revealing Reality (God) or the thing-in-itself, has called for tacit generalization from extraordinary occurrences in consciousness as well as that very use of the inferential method – it can only be that for those outside the orbit of such occurrences – that had been criticized in Schleiermacher. True phenomenology must be based on the valley of the everyday, constant, ordinary consciousness which apprehends itself by itself rather than by means of a numinous event, taking into consideration that for it the ideas of God and the soul are only dim and remote constructs, something outside, perhaps real and perhaps not real.

However, the numinous theory is very far from being wrong; in fact, quite the contrary. Its validity can be fully defended if its bounds are recognized. It is to be understood as a special theory of mystical consciousness rather than as a general theory of religious consciousness. But numinous occurrences can and must be enshrined in and mediated through religious sholes, assuming, therefore, an inevitable symbolic status so that they really express something to those who have had to limit their acquiantance – which means most people – with the holy to participation in mythic accounts, to reading or other usual means of contact with the experiences deposited in the memory of mankind, supplemented perhaps by some kinds of ritual or even intellectual re-enactment.

G. VAN DER LEEUW

G. van der Leeuw is a phenomenologist in the currently accepted sense as he has placed himself consciously within the stream of that tradition and has depended for Methodological purpose upon the fathers of the modern Phenomenological Movement like Husserl. Unlike Otto, he does not seek to break through the Kantian, agnostic boundary, for he observes, 'phenomenology aims not at things, still less at their mutual relations, and least of all at "the thing in itself".'[11]

A brief resumé of van der Leeuw's phenomenological method is in order. Phenomenology, as the term itself clearly suggests, is the study or discussion of what appears.[12] Appearance is a subject-object relation so that the phenomenon is an appearance to 'someone', and phenomenology concerns the relation to the 'someone' to whom the phenomenon appears. The method thus involves the study of both aspects of the relation between the 'object' that appears and the 'subject' to whom it appears. This relation engenders three levels of phenomenality, viz., the (relative) concealment of the phenomenon, its gradually becoming revealed and its transparency, and correlated with these (though not equivalent) three levels of life, viz., experience, understanding and testimony. More specifically speaking, understanding and testimony 'when systematically or scientifically employed constitute the procedure of phenomenology'.[13] Professor van der Leeuw stresses understanding as his central theme and indeed it is the goal of his search. Understanding corresponds to structure, which is 'the sketching of an outline within the chaotic maze of so-called "reality".'[14] Structure, in turn, is not what is either merely experienced or abstracted logically or causally but what is *understood*. In fact it is nothing other than the outlined complex of the relation between the phenomenon that appears and the person to whom it appears. It is reality significantly organized. But significance, in its turn, belongs in part to reality itself and in part to the 'someone' who attempts to understand it.[15] For this structure principle van der Leeuw has depended, as he himself implies, on Dilthey as well as on the psychologists Spranger and Binswanger.

Understanding leads one to the sphere of meaning as characterized by the event of understanding, which is what dawns upon us. '[Thus] the sphere of meaning is a third realm, subsisting above mere subjectivity and mere objectivity. The entrance gate to the reality of primal experience, itself wholly inaccessible, is *meaning: my* meaning and *its* meaning, which have become irrevocably one is the act of understanding.'[16] Although van der Leeuw is conscious of the excessive emphasis often laid on 'empathy' *(Einfühlung)* he himself, nevertheless, characterizes understanding as a symbolic re-living of the primal experience, a kind of thorough reconstruction, which, however, is to be safeguarded by rigorous hermeneutics of sacred texts, from degenerating into 'a pure art or empty fantasy'.[17] He conceives phenomenology to be, rather than a method, a truly vital activity 'that is distinctively human – not shared by either animal or god – of standing aside and understanding what appears into view'.[18] This entails in his thinking, as in that of other descriptive phenomenologists, bracketing, or exercising *epoché* with regard to whatever is behind the phenomenon. Max Scheler is quoted as saying:

'To be human means to hurl a forcible 'No' at this sort of reality. Buddha realized this when he said how magnificent it is to *contemplate* everything, and how terrible it is to *be:* Plato, too, in connecting the contemplation of ideas to a diverting of the soul from the sensuous content of objects, and to the diving of the soul into its own depths, in order to find the 'origins' of things. Husserl, also, implies nothing different than this when he links the knowledge of ideas with 'phenomenological reduction' – that is a 'crossing through' or 'bracketing' of (the accidental) coefficients of the existence of objects in the world in order to obtain their essentia.'[19]

Apparently, this method of *epoche* is a safeguard for the man who seeks understanding against his losing himself in either the things or the ego. While this is granted, it may be suggested as a modification, however, that *epoché* should be distinguished into two modes, namely, bracketing *in* and bracketing *out*, as already indicated in a previous place. Bracketing by itself is devoid of force and clarity. An idea like that of Ultimate Reality, which is supposed to be behind what appears (as distinct from its own essence), although impossible to be known, must be bracketed *in* and continue to have a special place in phenomenological inquiry. Without asking the unanswerable, philosophy is bound to breakdown. Phenomenology must consider the phenomena in their entire depth. As Karl Jaspers writes, 'Philosophy illuminates the mystery and brings it completely into consciousness.'[20] Hence the knowable and unattainable are to be meditated upon, not of course directly as part of the activity of phenomenology but indirectly, as *the absent* (which implies a very special kind of existence, continuous with all transcendent meaning) since it is a central constituent of certain phenomena which makes them what they are. This is a matter of great importance for phenomenology of religion, which will suggest that descriptiveness is not enough.

It seems that van der Leeuw after proceeding on the lines of pure descriptive phenomenology comes to a point where he realizes its limitations in the study of religion in another respect. Hence he observes: 'Phenomenology is the systematic discussion of what appears. Religion, however, is an ultimate experience that evades our observation, a revelation which in its very essence is, and remains, concealed. But how shall I deal with what is thus ever elusive and hidden? How can I pursue phenomenology when there is no phenomenon? How can I refer to phenomenology of religion at all?'[21]

The problem arises because in speaking about religion he has been, inadvertently perhaps, always on the side of theology rather than phenomenology, in spite of his declaration that he would not 'convert phenomenol-ogy to theology'.[22] His concern for revelation is legitimate enough, for without it as an Archimedean point religion cannot be religion. But phenom-enology as such, as van der Leeuw expects, cannot permit itself to arrive at 'conclusions concerning revelation itself' even indirectly or *per viam negationis*.[23] It seems that van der Leeuw quits dealing with religion in the true sense phenomenologically, despite his belief to the contrary. Where epistemology of religion is concerned his method, as clearly indicated by his own words, is hardly different from that of Otto, except that he employs the concept of *power* as denotation for 'the wholly Other', 'the Holy'.[24] Otto, on the contrary, by not speaking the language of phenomenology retains a higher degree of consistency as a chiefly theological thinker committed to his own clearly expressed goal of knowledge. As a phenomeno-logist, van der Leeuw holds on to *epoché* concerning God, Reality, but as a theologian, supplements it with faith, and he does not see them as mutually inconsistent.[25] Therefore, his programme of understanding has had to be radically revised. For, 'how indeed' he asks, 'can we understand what wholly eludes our understanding?'[26] This revision consists in substituting under-standing with 'becoming understood'. He observes, '[In other words]: the more deeply comprehension penetrates any event, and the better it "under-stands" it, the clearer it becomes to the understanding mind that the ultimate ground of understanding lies not within itself, but in some "other" from which it is comprehended from beyond the frontier.'[27] True enough, but the question is, will phenomenology not be really what it aims to be when instead of being concerned with 'the other' as such it is concerned with human consciousness which specifically in the way of being religious demands and responds to 'the other' (or some other form of self-transcendence as well) in order to be truly itself? For this to be the case one should first of all have bracketed *in* rather than *out* 'the other', God (or whatever is metaphysically perceived as transcendence). This way an about-turn could be avoided and the quest for phenomenological understanding of religion could be main-tained in the spirit of the struggle for human self-knowledge. The despair that van der Leeuw experiences about applying phenomenology to religion arises from the fact that he seems to have failed to perceive the distinction between two goals he entertains, namely, understanding of religion as phenom-enon and the understanding of the transcendent that that phenomenon reveals. The answer lies not in passing unnoticed from one to the other, but in re-investing the latter as a special fact within the former, in other words, in bracketing it *in*. If such a course is followed, the truth question in revelation will not have to be subjected to either rejection or premature evaluation – and evaluation is always premature in phenomenology – but could be entertained as something to be seriously contemplated, and only contemplated, within the structure of consciousness.

MIRCEA ELIADE

Mircea Eliade is a prolific contemporaray writer who has put forward a plethora of ideas significant for the comparative study of religion. Although it is not easy to summarize his thought, we can focus on some leading ideas that stand out and appear repeatedly in his writings. The first to be noted is the sacred which he believes to be the key to all life, expressed in the form of myth. But it has also a dialectic which has given rise to the notion of the profane. The study of religion as a phenomenon is therefore based on problems of the sacred versus the profane; every problem of life has to be analysed in terms of it in order that meaning may be discovered or made possible. The achievement of meaning is the same as the attainment of freedom.

The meaning and freedom issues, particularly as they are related to the predicament of modern man, introduce an existential dimension already present throughout Eliade's thinking. It may be said with accuracy that even his phenomenology of the sacred is pressed into service in resolving what he believes to be the central existential problem of modern man, namely the terror of history. So he writes:

'For the *Bhagavadgītā* as in some measure for Christianity the problem presented itself in these terms: How shall we resolve the paradoxical situation created by the two-fold fact that man, on the one hand, finds himself in *time*, given over to history, and on the other he knows that he will be 'damned' if he allows himself to be exhausted by temporality and historicity; that, consequently, he must at all costs find *in this world* a road that issues upon a transhistorical and atemporal plane?'[28]

This problem forces him to resort to a typology of the archaic over against the modern. The archaic, it must be remembered, is a typological category and does not mean simply old; likewise is also the modern. Of the archaic, India is accepted as the prime example as among its many virtues is the fact that it is still a very living tradition with a great wealth of philosophical and spiritual material, a complete whole by itself. The contemporary West quite naturally is shown to represent the modern, which unquestionably is also in process of relentlessly enveloping the whole world. Eliade's comparative study, therefore, is clearly cast in the mould of the archaic and modern spiritualities seen in the light of each other.

From this particular perspective, Eliade launches an extensive study of various cultures and religions, and his goals appear to be the following: (1) To discover how archaic cultures provided defenses against history 'either by periodically abolishing it through repetition of cosmogony and a periodical regeneration of time or by giving historical events a meta-historical meaning, a meaning that was not only consoling but was above all coherent, that is capable of being fitted into a well-consolidated system in which the cosmos and man's existence had each its raison d'être'.[29] (2) To realize that modern man is without defense against history, while its terror becomes 'more and more intolerable from the viewpoint afforded by the various historicistic philosophies (like Hegel's)',[30] and to realize also that 'as existence becomes more and more precarious because of history, the positions of historicism will increasingly lose in prestige and humanity will desist from any further "making of history".'[31] (3) To grasp a source of freedom from this terror caused by man's 'presence in the historical universe' rather than by 'his own human existentiality'.[32] Here Eliade seems to point to two completely different sources of freedom, one consisting in Yoga, essentially the greatest refinement and the epitome of the archaic itself, and the other in a variation of the modern expressed in prophetic Christianity. Each of them in its own way would ensure freedom.

Yoga, it is pointed out, 'is a survival of the archaic spirituality that survived nowhere else'.[33] The symbolism of birth and rebirth present in its initiatory structure, along with some other things, provide evidence of archaism.[34] 'For Yoga', he concludes, 'the initiatory rebirth becomes the acquisition of immortality or absolute freedom', 'a paradisaical state' that can take man out of profane existence'.[35] A different approach to freedom appears in (modern) Christianity, which by definition is 'the religion of modern man'.[36] In Eliade's words:

'Since the invention of faith, in the Judaeo-Christian sense of the word (= for God all is possible), the man who has left the horizon of archetypes and repetition can no longer defend himself against that terror (of history) except through the idea of God. In fact it is only by presupposing the existence of God that the conquers, on the one hand, freedom (which grants him autonomy in a universe governed by laws, or in other words, the 'inauguration' of a mode of being that is new and unique in the universe) and, on the other hand, the certainty that historical tragedies have a trans-historical meaning, even if that meaning is not always visible for humanity in its present condition. Any other situation of modern man leads in the end to despair.'[37]

Professor Eliade has made his position very clear and leaves us is no doubt as to his objectives. But what is difficult to comprehend is how he proposes to make a path to freedom formed in one context, the archaic that is, viable in a totally different one, namely, the modern. He suggests that one of the Western man's concerns in studying Yoga (or all Eastern and archaic religions by extension) is to see 'what solution India proposes for the anxiety produced by our discovery of our temporality and historicity, the means by which one can remain in the world without letting oneself be exhausted by time and history'.[38] There is first of all a formal contradiction here, as Eliade while proposing this also simultaneously defines the archaic and the modern as so different as to be almost mutually exclusive. But we must not dwell on the formal logical aspect of the matter but take up something nearer home to our present interest.

In Eliade's scheme the principal focus is the practical aspect of gaining freedom from anxiety, which Yoga represents in one way and faith in another. There are obvious similarities between Eliade's scheme and the one underlying this essay but with the following differences: (1) We propose two types of spiritualities represented by the specifically Indian and Western religious traditions rather than by the archaic and the modern; and we consider the modern as something to be genetically located in the latter. (And strictly as types they can make no claim to exhaust the world of possibilities, but are really only types which as such rather than extinguish might even enkindle others). (2) We conceive anxiety and tranquillity as keys to these types of spiritualities, both equally revelatory of human consciousness, and hence equally significant phenomenologically. (And we consistently take care that these categories remain at the phenomenological level as we understand it and never trespass into that of metaphysics). And as our interest lies in knowing, rather than in effectuating release, we are forbidden to set up the tranquillity structures as an answer to the upsurges of anxiety, as indeed does Eliade. (3) While we admit that the search for freedom from anxiety will continue to be made, and ever more desperately, we note the unlikelihood of a contact with the real essence of the tranquillity traditions in religion at a significantly deep level. (4) We assume that both anxiety and tranquillity have their reasons for being, in fact have their own ontologies resident in consciousness, with the qualification that that of the former is far more concealed and paradoxical than that of the latter. This being so, their essential mutuality is such that it can be manifested only in the passivity of the two being apprehended together in thought. However, in the divided world of the spirit they must and will resist each other till the end of time, while also dialectically comprehending each other. (5) We deal with anxiety not as problem to be solved or as ill to be eliminated but as *problematic*, that is to say, as the mechanism by which consciousness recognizes and poses to itself *the* fundamental problem which is none other than existence, history being at once both a condition and a product of its specific modality, the only one that is known to us. (6) We work under the calculation that the dialectic between anxiety structures and tranquillity structures is going to be one of the most important dramas in mankind's spiritual future. And while obviously it cannot take place in the realms of the merely abstract, the concrete forms of the spiritual life, that is to say, the particular religious traditions, will cease to be the sole custodians of these structures. The boundaries of the religions will even dissolve to an extent but their disembodied spirits – continuing through the types of spiritualities – will be just as powerful. Perhaps a new, unorthodox, purely voluntaristic membership pattern in these types might emerge, signs of which already abound. But the new will never be the same as the old in so far as there will have been a mutual awareness of the two structures as the context for any spiritual decision and consequently some inevitable mutual influences although mostly external. The tranquillity of one who has known anxiety can only be a tranquillity in quest of itself and hence is different from that of another who has been spiritually shielded from anxiety. (7) We discount the practical value of seeking freedom from modern anxiety structures through the rediscovery of an archaic spirituality; and in its place we substitute an intellectual value, one that consists in knowing and knowing deeply. (8) We take the position that anxiety is not to be looked upon as something that *occurs* at the level of *individual* life, as then it is likely to suggest superficial solutions, but as something that *resides* at the *universal* level of being from which it manifests itself in individual psyche and through it in society and civilization. The inability to heed the call of being to universal anxiety and penetrate it brings about a certain individualized, neurotic form of it concerning all things ranging downward from death and life, most of all concerning the impossibility of having, facing and knowing true anxiety itself. Anxiety, in fact, at its ultimate depth contains its own solution or its own potentiality for genuine tranquillity, in other words, 'peace that passeth understanding', to be apprehended in no other way than through a baptism of anxiety. (Jesus asked his disciples, 'Can you ... be baptized with the baptism that I am baptized with?', Mark 10:38). There is such a thing as *holy* anxiety or the saint's anxiety, between which and the essence of the tranquillity tradition an authentic commerce would become possible. One must, therefore, walk with one's gaze fixed on that goal while bathing one's symbols of knowledge and experience in true anxiety and true tranquillity which are mediated through everything that the revelations stand for.

In substance, our position is that where ultimate questions of existence are concerned we may have no recourse to take but in thinking, contemplating. Regardless of the images of futility and even unreality that these words arouse in most people's minds, they are more true to life in that they hold up a mirror before it not excluding the real futility of those measures which are supposed to eventuate in practical results. There should, however, not arise any fear that thought will discredit faith or Yoga as means to freedom. All it does is to help them achieve critical self-understanding so that by reaching the boundaries of practicality by fore-knowledge their inherent epistemological elements will be released. Hence there is no real prospect of an opposition between thought and these other things. Thought has the advantage of perceiving the limitations of all means, itself included. Its saving grace is that it can think not only of everything else but of itself also. This being the case the vain temptation of some forms of rationalist philosophy to equate thought with Reality should never really arise.[39] In any case the function of thought vis-à-vis Ultimate Reality does not even become a problem in this strictly phenomenological inquiry. Even the self-knowledge that is sought is purely of a phenomenological character.

But such self-knowledge itself is not conceived as anything other than penetrating the symbolic by means of the symbolic. It is assumed that all our knowledge and experiences are sheathed in symbols. As Cassirer observes: 'No longer can man confront reality immediately; he cannot see it, as it were, face to face... He has so enveloped himself in linguistic forms, in artistic images, in mythical symbols or religious rites that he cannot see or know anything except by the interposition of this artificial medium. His situation is the same in the theoretical as in the practical sphere.'[40] This must apply to existential self-knowledge also so that one's own ultimate perceptions of oneself cannot break loose from the symbolic circle that surrounds the sphere of human existence. When we speak of anxiety and the terror of history we should be aware that they do not reach us except as they are filtered through many sieves as it were, all of them being symbols erected by the psyche, society and life itself. To an extent some 'insane' persons who, to whatever degree become bereft of the uses of those protective screens, are relatively, although spasmodically, more open to terror and anxiety;[41] and on the other end of the scale are the god-men chosen for it, who know the ultimate anxiety of existence really, non-symbolically and in their infinite depths, whose knowledge become reference points for all men, in other words, constituents of certain revelations. Such universal reference points mediated this wise do not, however, mitigate the symbolic character of our own experiences but rather open up deeper dimensions of meaning and provide symbolic gauges for measuring the immeasurable. Clearly, revelation by definition has to do with the transcendent, and the depth of awareness present in the god-men does surpass the boundaries of phenomenological understanding, while what is within its scope are those symbolic forms apprehended in revelation.

We can achieve self-knowledge only through a thought that is not shy to use all the symbolic forms and is courageous – and humble – enough to accept its own character as an activity dealing with symbols. If man should know himself, thought too should know itself. The real, non-symbolic depth of man's being is not knowable to him; by hypothesis whoever can know it becomes more than man, namely a god or god-man. To remain content to be a thinker is to affirm one's humanity. This of course, does not mean that he is freed from the necessity to perform acts that all must perform. But he will know that such acts, however noble, are essentially of a ritual character. Striving for freedom from anxiety or history is ritual too, even if sometimes and in special ways they are also effective techniques. The thinker is not fooled by their effectiveness. Whenever man moves towards the ultimate he is performing ritual acts (even if they are thought acts) as the steps in his movement are always immediate while he is forced to fancy that their fruits are ultimate, which, if it were the case, would posit an infinite gap that could never be bridged by proximate steps. But as he regains his self-awareness he moves towards himself through the symbols controlled by thought. Anxiety and tranquillity as both inhabiting the depth of consciousness and as nuclei for manifest structures of man's spiritual life become revealed to us through symbols and symbols only.

6

Consciousness and Religion

CONSCIOUSNESS' REFLECTION UPON ITSELF: THE FACT AND THE METHOD
DISTINGUISHED

Modern philosophy is indebted to Edmund Husserl for providing it with
a new starting-point in the study of consciousness. All contemporary phenomenology whether concerned with religion or any other area of investigation,
must, by remote or immediate dependence, be necessarily grounded in
Husserl's thought. It is needless nowadays to speak of Husserl's influence
upon later writers in this tradition as the writings of Max Scheler, Alfred
Schutz, Paul Tillich, J.-P. Sartre, M. Merleau-Ponty and Martin Heidegger
himself will loudly testify. The most revolutionary principle of all for which
many feel indebted to Husserl is the structure of intentional consciousness,
construed as the primordial link between consciousness and the world.[1]
The influence of his thought in the contemporary world extends also to the
comparative study of religion. G. van der Leeuw, as we have seen in the last
chapter, is one of the foremost scholars in the field of the phenomenology
of religion who drew heavily from Husserl.

  The broad assumption of this method is something very simple, in different
ways expressed by others before. But Husserl made it the bedrock of a novel
way of thinking, demonstrating persuasively that consciousness is the primary datum, a datum to itself, upon which must be based a whole new systematic enterprise in philosophy. The manifesto for this new systematic activity of thought can be discerned in the following statement of Husserl's:
'[Thus] we fix our eyes steadily upon the sphere of Consciousness and study
what it is that we find immanent in *it*. At first, without having carried out the
phenomenological suspensions of the element of judgment, we subject this
sphere of Consciousness in its essential nature to a systematic though in no
sense exhaustive analysis. What we lack above all is a certain general insight

into the essence of *consciousness in general*, and quite specifically also of consciousness, so far as in and through its essential Being the 'natural' fact-world comes to be known. In these studies we go as far as is needed to furnish the full insight at which we have been aiming, to wit *that consciousness in itself has a being of its own which in its absolute uniqueness of nature remains unaffected by the phenomenological disconnexion*. It therefore remains over as a *phenomenological residuum*, as a region of Being which is in principle unique and can become in fact the field of a new science – the science of phenomenology.'[2]

Consciousness and reflection go together. Husserl links them thus: '"It" (*reflexion*, which we prefer to write simply as reflection) is as we may also express it, the name we give to consciousness' own method for the knowledge of consciousness generally.' 'But', he adds, 'in this very method it *(reflexion)* itself becomes the object of possible studies.'[3] The numerous aspects of this method of reflection, particularly with regard to retention, memory, to the 'living now' etc.,[4] although very important for its full understanding, should not command our attention in our own restricted investigation. But notice must be taken of the great significance that Husserl himself assigned to it as he observes:

'The fundamental methodological importance for phenomenology, and no less for psychology, of reflexions in their essential nature is manifest in this, that under the concept of reflexion must be included all modes of immanent apprehension of the essence, and on the other hand all modes of immanent experience *(Erfahrung)*. So, for instance, the immanent perception, which in point of fact is a reflexion, in so far as it presupposes a shifting of the glance from something we are conscious of objectively to the subjective consciousness of it.'[5]

Now, there will arise the question when we link consciousness and reflection, what different meanings may be attached to the latter. Philosophers have used the word 'reflection' throughout the ages, as it is indispensable for philosophy. But none of the traditional meanings are relevant for our purpose for the simple reason that, in contrast to phenomenology, there is in them no special conception of linking reflection with consciousness. This declaration will suffice to remove all feeling of obligation to study the various uses of the word in the history of philosophy, and help to retain it for the specific sense in which it has been intended.

However, one particular distinction which often lies unnoticed in phenomenology, and which most writers in that tradition by-pass, is one between reflection as a *fact* of consciousness itself, as a spontaneous self-activity, and reflection as a method of studying phenomena, beginning with and indeed depending on, consciousness. The latter is much more apparent than the former in Husserl's method, summarized in the phrase: 'Back to things themselves'. The novelty of this method consists in the uniqueness of the way one goes about making a science of what manifests it self to us *(legein ta phainomena)* in order to know the things themselves, by-passing, perhaps even surpassing, the realism-agnosticism syndrome in traditional metaphysics.[6] It promises, at least in Heidegger's version, the being of be-ings *(das Sein des Seienden)*.[7]

This concerns the controversy latent in the difference between Husserl and Heidegger as to whether phenomenology must be restricted to the being of consciousness only or to be extended to being as such. But we must completely side-step this argument. Rather, our query must be directed towards the structure of intentional consciousness, in the spirit of which most phenomenologists tend to understand reflection in the methodological sense only to the virtual neglect of reflection in the sense of the spontaneous self-activity of consciousness.

In respect of the query thus addressed, it must in all fairness to Husserl, be said that phenomena were not to be confined in his presentation to things that appear to the senses but to works of art, technique, etc., for he lays down: 'We busy ourselves ... with the essential nature of *consciousness of something* following for instance, our consciousness of the existence of material things, living bodies and men, or that of technical and literary works, and so forth.'[8] As a starting-point he would 'take consciousness in a pregnant sense which suggests itself at once, most simply indicated by the Cartesian *cogito*, I think'.[9] But nowhere does he appear to make consciousness as it reflects upon itself as the subject of further reflection. In fact consciousness of other things seems to be inhibited by consciousness of consciousness and this inhibition is not the same as *cogito*. This being the case the extension of the structure of intentional consciousness so as to include also deliberate reflection upon the spontaneous and innate self-activity of reflecting upon itself would seem to be warranted by the method. Phenomenology's justification for starting with consciousness rather than with the phenomena outside it is that it is itself a unique phenomenon, one that is always in the process of apprehending itself along with its own states (or moods), and by that means, of apprehending the world (or being of be-ings).

Thus, two very important truths present themselves to us: (1) There is a first-order reflection, a spontaneous activity of consciousness directed towards itself as well as a second-order reflection, a methodological activity of consciousness initiated by the thinker. (2) These two orders are connected, which is a fact that the methodological thinker must always bring to greater clarity. In the light of these truths it may be concluded that while it is quite legitimate for phenomenology to make consciousness as it apprehends everything in the world – all phenomena – as a prerequisite for the study of everything, it is obligated to itself to reflect also on consciousness as it reflects upon itself, or, so to say, involuntarily tries to apprehend itself and thereby confront existence. Heidegger would heartily concede this although he does not use the language of the two orders of reflection but there is a reason why we want to use it, which will be made apparent straightaway.

Our hope is that by elucidating the concept of the first-order reflection of consciousness upon itself and by subjecting it to the second-order (methodological) reflection a rather novel possibility for the study of religion will be unfolded, which will be different from what phenomenologists of religion have hitherto developed. Accordingly, we seek to locate religion in the particular self-activity of consciousness, which stands out, with no intent. however, to exclude other elements of consciousness pointed to by thinker, like Rudolf Otto which have also their places in the manifestation of religions It is necessary that consciousness be made transparent to itself by removing all opacities that obstruct its self-disclosure. When Husserl speaks of transcendental consciousness – as against all other kinds of transcendental entities, including God, which he argues must be suspended, the implicit emphasis is on the removal of all obstructions from consciousness so that, theoretically speaking, it will be disclosed as its own irreducible ground.[10]

Consciousness being subjected to this kind of study would reveal an intrinsic and inalienable character of it, which can be interpreted only by the key of religion. Husserl has allowed the possibility of a phenomenology of religion as of several other facts only on condition that a 'disconnection from Nature' will be achieved concomitantly.[11] While the legitimacy of this demand must be granted, as far as religion is concerned the disconnection must be pushed one step further back, because it, unlike state, moral custom and law, and even more drastically, unlike the varieties of cultural expressions, is more internal to the self and hence must be predicated upon consciousness' reflection upon itself. A certain character of consciousness will be revealed as plenary to the coming into being of the 'phenomenon' of religion and perhaps also, by one step removed, to the manifestation of other 'natural realities' like state, moral custom and law. This character does not conflict with other elements of consciousness like the numinous sense, feeling of dependence and ultimate concern which are pointed out by different thinkers as the source of religion, but, on the contrary, will feed into them and be integrated with them. It will be seen to be universal and pervasive, resident in the self-activity of consciousness.

THE SENSE OF WRONGNESS OF EXISTENCE

As consciousness reflects upon itself – and it always does – there arises a sense pertaining to existence which indicates that it, as it is given, is somehow wrong and not right. The self-confrontation of existence takes place in consciousness' reflection upon itself. This sense of wrongness cannot be truly explained as a matter of constitution since in actual life there never is encountered an alternative way of constituting the self or projecting existence. The only alternatives that are possible come in the form of myth which in turn are grounded on the sense of wrongness itself as an answer, remedy, solution, offering a structure of rectification. The sense of wrongness of existence is not to be understood as an ordinary discontent that can be removed by some special argument or analysis or knowledge, although quests in that direction are automatically launched from this ground. It should be assumed that it is as fundamental as wonder and curiosity which are regarded respectively as the sources of philosophy and science. It engenders not only theoretical but also practical activities as, on the one hand, it demands to be interpreted, causally, or teleologically perhaps, in that it governs the irremovable ground of self-awareness, and, on the other, calls for its resolution or overcoming in some way in order to make transcendence of it both conceivable and possible.

Consciousness' reflection upon itself is to be regarded as neither adventitious nor optional but essential, and instances of consciousness totally free of it and hence devoid of the sense of wrongness have never been encountered in actual life, and if it has to exist it has to be invented. The degree of variation in intensity in self-reflection among individuals is in itself immaterial, self-reflection being ultimately a universal, social fact, operating as a social fact exactly in the manner of myth, ritual and symbolism, which are incidentally themselves used as vehicles for its self-expression.[12] In this respect every individual instance of self-awareness and the socially immanent general self-awareness reinforce each other. And such denials of the sense of wrongness as a fact that are sometimes made, for instance by some naturalists, pragmatists and positivists, are unquestionably the result of philosophical attitudes formed in a spirit of defiance and consequently are to be treated as implicit answers to the fact already apprehended a priori but not admitted to.

It must be clearly recognized that consciousness by its very nature is subjective, but the subjectivity of consciousness must be extended so as in principle to comprehend all instances of its occurrence. It is the nature of conscious entities to seek other entities like themselves, and this can be done only by objectivising the path of meeting. But such objectivisation is only provisional and the possibility and the necessity of overcoming it are embedded in it. Most of all, conscious entities have the power of recognizing all other conscious entities in themselves subjectively as well as in others objectively. In this path neither the absurdity of solipsism and hence of denying the world of all subjects nor that of the subject becoming an object and getting lost in a world of objective 'things' will become a real threat. The subject will know itself as both perceiver and perceived simultaneously. And finally the sense of wrongness of existence will be verified both internally and externally in reflection. However, religion already accomplishes these movements of consciousness by its own spontaneous self-activity of reflection. This is the primal stuff out of which religion is woven. Methodological or second-order reflection is required only to retrace the steps by which the original act of reflection takes place and hence so to say, re-enact religion in explicit thought and thus bring it to the level of understanding.

There cannot, however, be a complete phenomenology of religion based solely upon the fact of consciousness' reflection upon itself and the sense of wrongeness. An effort in that direction should be judged as immoderate and antithetical to the demand for an integral theory implicit in the phenomenon itself. Nevertheless, in this approach there is an effort to supply a certain essential element, a vital dynamic, that has been missed out by all other theories including the phenomenological ones. Paul Elmer More was giving utterance to a greater truth than he knew when he suggested some years ago that for making a viable theory of religion 'we must fall back from our standpoint upon some element of consciousness which is universal to all men and cannot honestly be disputed'.[13] Our effort here at least tries to respect that great truth. It has undoubtedly much in common with many contemporary expressions – in literature, philosophy and art – of existential thought. But as a rule and perhaps unavoidably, these expressions come in highly specified forms, for example, in such notions as the absurd, nausea, alienation and *angst* (the last in its very highly precise ontological formulation). The sense of the wrongness of existence upon which a view of religion has to be based, by the very nature of the case, cannot afford to be as specific as any of them but must be vague and general enough to comprehend all of them as it also receives confirmation of itself through their instrumentality. Among the theories of religion put forward as such there are some that have marginal affinity with ours. One of these to be singled out is what is contained in a book put out not long ago by Martin P. Nilsson under the title, *Religion as Man's Protest Against the Meaninglessness of Events*. The thesis of the book is expressed in the title itself. Nilsson too seeks only a modest role for his theory as he is aware, like us, of the complexity of the phenomenon of religion and in that spirit declares, 'In saying that religion is a protest against the meaninglessness of events I wish only to emphasize one side of the various aspects of religion and to try to see what its importance is'.[14] He points out that there are different kinds of events, and likewise different kinds of protests, some that in the very form of protest constitute also a way of realizing meaning in the meaningless through ritual, myth and even thought. Death is shown to be the most important of these meaning-robbing events which as much dominated the primitive mind as it does the modern.[15]

In constructing a general phenomenology of religion based on that aspect of consciousness revealed as the sense of wrongness, we must be mindful of the need of a scale which moves from the most general and objectified levels of it right up to the very high, exceptional levels, shared only by the very few. The appearance of these very few occurs in a paradoxical fashion, for on the one hand they have to participate intensely in this particular reality of society that we are concerned with – as obviously in others too – and, on the other, seem to need to stand outside of society itself in order to be able to do so. This means that they have to interiorize the forms of wrongness objectified in society as myth, ritual and symbol and yet by using them as ladders tend to surpass society itself. Such a paradoxical double movement must finally come to rest only in that consummation called vicariousness, where an individual stands in the place of society and fulfills it by surpassing it. It is also true, contrariwise, that society must seek to transcend itself by configuring such images, obviously through qualified seers and spokesmen. These truths are very powerfully echoed in the words of Second Isaiah 'Surely he hath borne our griefs and carried our sorrows'.[16] In society the sense of wrongness is present only in a generalized form, encrusted over, terminated and constantly suppressed by life. The exceptional, direct awareness of the few also returns to and is stored again, in the objectified structures of myth, ritual and symbol in society. The role of descriptive phenomenology must be expanded so as to be of service in understanding these facts.

THE ABSENT

The sense of the wrongness of existence is always attended by an equally generalized and abiding sense of an Absent Reality, often appearing as an Absent Divine. This latter sense is probably none other than the awareness of being (or Being) and joy vitiated by the all-pervading sense of wrongness. And every presentness, even presentness of the Divine, must be cast in the mould of the Absent, which is the first-order reflection's own way of bracketing being (Being), subsequently to be replayed by the methodological reflection of phenomenology. Therefore, what the latter of the two reflections accomplishes is nothing but travelling the same road a second time that was taken by the former.

To call the Absent One, God (in whatever way, namely, polytheistically, monotheistically or absolutistically) is the culmination to which one arrives by walking the path of myth; to call it Nothing is to depart from that path. But calling it Nothing can be done in two diverse ways, that is to say, either in the manner of interrogation, evocation and intensified protest, or in that of a terminal dogma. The former way is not antithetical to reverence, humility, while the latter way is, and betrays arrogance.

The sense of the wrongness of existence arises, no doubt, against an ontic background, upon which existence is projected as upon a screen. But the interplay of the background and the projection presents only an elusive shadow of which the substance would for ever seem to be there by being not there, that is to say, by appearing that it ought to exist on one consideration but absolutely cannot on another. The shadow is a cosmos-sized one, nay larger than the cosmos, which it encloses, and simply presents an image the interior of which is thoroughly blotted out. What the image itself does is to provide an outline to mark the absence of Reality. And wherever we look there we see the outlines of the image and within the outlines the Absent One.[17] However, if the phenomenology of the Absent is made to serve the ends of some mystical technique or some theological doctrine implied in the *via negativa* then it will have missed its ultimate purpose. While the legitimacy of efforts of that kind may be granted under certain conditions, the Absent must never be exhausted by them, and indeed must eternally be on its guard against them. As the Absent is the resting place of religion in the final analysis, the two together must defend themselves on their own ground against both mysticism and theology. The absence of God has been one of the great themes of modern religious and philosophical thought, particularly in the Western tradition. The Death of God theology is one of its expressions, but in that form, that is, in the garb of theology, the theme really loses its meaning as it reveals itself as an ingenious but ungenuine instrument of apologetics. And as for unqualified mystical use of the theme equally strong disapprobation has to be expressed. Simone Weil, a profound thinker, it is widely known, had much to say on the Absent. Her words, 'We have to believe in a God who is like the true God in everything except that he does not exist', are memorable. But whether utterances like this could be construed as forming the core of what one writer calls 'a mysticism of atheistic purification',[18] is a matter of great consequence – and of some doubt. But whatever be the truth with respect to Miss Weil's position, it may be said that the Absent must resist mysticism, as it must resist theology, in the definitive form. But this should, however, not mean that it can throw its door wide open to the negatively sanctimonious self-certainty of official scepticism.

In opposition to both the alternatives it must simply stand on its own ground and continue to abide with itself. The phenomenology of the Absent is neither the mysticism nor the theology of the Absent. Nevertheless, we must also exclude the purely ontological aspect of the question from this essay, but must take note of the fact that among the thinkers gripped by it Heidegger himself is the foremost.[19] But out of necessity we must elude capture by the ontological inquiry.

THE EXPRESSION OF CONSCIOUSNESS THROUGH THE HISTORY OF RELIGION, AND THE EXEGESIS OF THE SENSE OF WRONGNESS

The ideas of the sense of the wrongness of existence and the attendant sense of the Absent must be treated as the most general presentations of what in the course of the historical development of religion and thought based on it have become specific and have been bodied forth in specific types of existential awareness and specific formulations of Reality. Correspondingly, there have also developed specific approaches to righting that which is wrong. (Two very clearly different types of all these are what we shall attempt to outline in the immediately succeeding chapters.) For instance, every movement of contemporary existentialism has some interpretation of wrongness and of reality as determined by its religious sources. But to try to give an exposition of any would be rather redundant since discussions of this kind are plentiful in today's literature. But one must point also to another sphere where a different set of expressions of wrongness and of reality, as specific as the Western, are present. The Buddha's insistence on the universal fact of suffering *(duḥkha)* is well-known; in truth all Indian religious systems assume the same standpoint although with less emphasis than the Buddha.

But ordinarily, in accounts of the genesis of such existential ideas in both the East and the West certain thinkers and thought-events are credited with originating them. Clearly, one fundamental issue in existential thinking is its own beginning or source. All thinking needs a beginning, which must spring from some fundamental 'primitive fact', 'a central reference point' as such thinkers as Merleau-Ponty and Eugen Fink, along with a host of others, point out.[20] It would be absurd to say that thinking can supply its own primitive fact or reference point. Or is it enough to admit, as Heidegger himself does, that thinking needs presuppositions?[21] Undoubtedly, Heidegger wanst to go beyond this and it is hard to see how he would give aid and comfort to those who make presuppositions arbitrary or a matter of wager. In Heidegger's belief the foundation of thought has to be discovered – quite rightly – and for this reason the exploration of being through *Dasein*, which is his principal objective, must be accompanied by a similar exploration of thought *(Denken)*. Under this rubric presupposition is in no danger of becoming a bland concept, it being conceived as the very disclosure of being in be-ings through *Dasein*. However, even this approach suffers from a two-fold defect: (1) It conducts itself as though religion has not existed; (2) *Dasein* upon which it depends, is constructed in a highly specific way and hence cannot be meaningful unless subjected to an equally specific hermeneutic as required. The specificity, obviously comes from its being exclusively a part of a single sphere of the spirit. But this predicament is shared by all expressions in philosophy and religion. It cannot be overcome, but can be subjected to understanding through comparative phenomenology.

But the really serious defect is the first one, which would not be noticeable in any thought that is less profound than Heidegger's. Hence we must turn to it. However, the discussion will not centre around Heidegger necessarily but around the existential thinkers' general apathy towards the history of religion and what it intimates. This is deemed serious because they fail to show a realm of life with which consciousness can establish correspondence in respect of the sense of wrongness even in its specific interpretations like *angst*, dread, alienation or the absurd. Analysis of consciousness without correspondence will not bear any concrete fruit; but with correspondence the beginning of thought, its source – at least of existential thought – can be uncovered as abiding in the sense of wrongness and of the Absent, whose universality may either be left in a state of undefined and primitive vagueness or be denoted specifically through any one of the alternative sets of existential categories.

By correspondence consciousness discovers itself in the realm of religion where it is fully imaged, and thought, existential thought, emanates from the tides of such self-discovery. In other words, the locus of thought is the point of mutual transition between consciousness and history of religion, our contention being that the latter too exists even for those who disavow it, and no man is free from it as no man is free from the self-reflection of consciousness – or from the law of gravity. The establishing of such correspondence is the real meaning of exegesis.

It is good to recognize that history of religion enshrines and carries the most fundamental ideas of mankind and the philosopher who studies the religions can study these ideas in their concrete expressions. Among the great philosophers it is Hegel, more than any one else, who was moved by this great insight and his work with all its limitations was a bold act of exegesis of the kind we are pleading for. One must be warned against deliberately disassociating oneself from such a living storehouse of ideas as the history of religion. In Heidegger's case, it has to be said that his well-known concern with such matters as history, history of philosophy, the lived world and mythology (the *logos* of the *mythos*) are by no means sufficient to make up for the neglect of the religious actualities. What is true of Heidegger is also true in varying degrees of other existentialist thinkers. A commitment to 'the mystery of being' or openness to theology will in itself not remedy this defect.

Heidegger, and following him, the Heideggerians, move between the realms of pure ontology (conceived in a special way so as to surpass older metaphysics, to be sure) and pure mythology and build an arch, so to say, over another terrain, that of the history of religion. Accordingly, the central category of religion, viz., revelation is approached either ontologically (sometimes onto-theologically) or mythologically with the result that it loses its authenticity and independence which are apprehensible from the standpoint of phenomenology. While a degree of legitimacy may be granted to these approaches, the prospect of exclusive mutual illumination – at the purely phenomenological level – between religion and revelation must never be lost sight of. By turning myth itself into revelation, or pro-revelation of Being as Walter Otto has it,[22] revelation is shifted from its primary realm of occurrence as a category and its meaning consequently altered. To be sure, the mythic form of revelation must be granted but the study of that is only the secondary task of phenomenology, its first task being always defined as the study of any category in the realm in which it primarily and essentially occurs. With the restoration of the history of religion to its own authentic domain a new possibility for philosophy, different from both ontology and the phenomenology of myth, will be unveiled. And where do we find religion and revelation? Not in the realm of pure contemplation or thought but in that of historic actuality. Clearly, religion is not exhausted by such historic entities as Christianity, Islam, Buddhism and Hinduism. True en ough, but neither can we know it without them. As for revelation, the problem of which revelation is true and which not does not arise at this level of inquiry. The phenomenological thinker as such can afford to be equanimous before the three-fold prospect, namely, (1) that all may be true, (2) that all may be false, (3) that some may be true and others false, (or perhaps that one may be true while others may be false). He needs only be concerned with its appearing as a category of knowledge within the context of the history of religion and as such he will establish the conditions for indirectly raising the question of ultimate truth, which is the only valid way to raise it. However, in respect of being, the comparative phenomenologist fulfills his special vocation by recognizing and becoming open to the multiple possibility governing it but without being directly involved in the destiny of any single one.

The theologians' desire to journey further on by a road where ontology and mythology intertwine is obviously comprehensible. But there are also some phenomenologists of religion who take the same road, one of the most notable today being Paul Ricœur. Ricœur primarily focusses attention on mythic consciousness, its unity, universality, pervasiveness and multiformity, along with the symbol which together form the ground from which man draws the power to reason. He argues that one must begin with the most inarticulate and spontaneous expressions of this consciousness rather than with its speculative and rational expressions.[23] He analyses further the primordial character of myth-making and the symbolic character of man. All this leads him to a central ontological thesis, namely, that some fault *(la faute)* reigns at the very heart of human reality. The ontology besides is one of will expressible in the equation, fault = fall = fallibility, which is analysed as a disposition of the will that is free.[24] In fact fallibility is the inclination of the will to evil. He argues that pure reflection even without the instrumentality of myth and symbol will take one to 'a certain threshold of intelligibility where the possibility of evil is inscribed in the innermost structure of human reality'.[25] Ricœur makes clear his dependence on Heidegger, Gabriel Marcel and also the theological tradition. Therefore his ontology involves him in an epistemology of 'confession' of evil and 'wager' after the manner of Pascal. He believes strongly in presupposition for philosophy but that is conceived as wager. So he writes, 'Such is the *wager*. Only he can object to this mode of thought who thinks that philosophy to begin with itself, must be a philosophy without presuppositions. A philosophy that starts from the fullness of language is a philosophy with presuppositions. To be honest, it must make its presuppositions explicit, state them as beliefs, wager on the beliefs, and try to make the wager pay off in understanding.'[26] There is no doubt that Ricœur leads the way to ultimately convert phenomenology to theology and in the effort to elucidate religion he makes one religion the norm for all. However, he is frank enough to confess that a phenomenology *oriented by* the Western quest alone 'cannot do justice to the great experiences of India and China', whose civilizations 'are of equal value with the Greek and Jewish civilizations'. But he concludes this perspective with the conditional and futuristic statement that 'the point of view from which this equality of value can be seen does not yet exist and it will exist only when a universal human culture has brought all cultures together in a whole'.[27] In the meantime he would accept a principle of limitation. In our case, on the contrary, our line of inquiry requires that we defy such limitations and await the command of consciousness, which alone can give direction to phenomenology.

7

Anxiety and Tranquillity: the Spheres of the Spirit

The Problem of Types

We have reached a stage in our inquiry into consciousness where we realize that we cannot advance any further unless we introduce the consideration of types. Comparative religion itself has employed typology in many ways according to the vision of the particular scholars concerned. Thus Nathan Söderblom, Rudolf Otto and G. van der Leeuw, among others, have their own typological principles but to discuss their virtues is entirely outside the scope of the present work. However, one thing may be said: any scholar who puts forward a typology with the expectation that it is going to be fool-proof must be labouring under an illusion. Type arrangements can be used only for very specific purposes, strictly for the sake of illuminating some issues and not as comprehensive schemes that can stand all tests.

This caution will have to be built into the scheme we suggest. However, there is a call for typology in view of the line of inquiry into consciousness that we have adopted. Our typology should be good enough to throw light on the path we have chosen to travel, and no more. It is not expected that it will illuminate other paths in comparative religious and philosophical studies. As Paul Tillich wisely observes: 'Types are logical ideals for the sake of discerning understanding.'[1] With this we agree in part and disagree also in part. We disagree to the extent that it implies that types are *only* logical ideals, especially as Tillich adds that 'they do not exist in time and space'. In fact, they exist both logically and concretely in certain historic spiritual spheres. But we should heartily endorse his vision of making seemingly static types dynamic. The programme of constructing a dynamic typology through the dialectical use of contrasting poles within one structure will be received with complete sympathy but in our division of topics it belongs to the dialogue issue and will be considered in that context. And we may by anticipation take heart from the thought that even the types that differ can become internal to the same individual's thinking.

Tillich, along with all other thinkers in the phenomenology of religion, anchors typology in types of religion. But in this study we seek to base typology on consciousness as we have decided to simultaneously move one step backward and one step forward from religion, in fact, in an effort to surround it entirely. Accordingly, we set up (1) something subtler and more hidden than religion, namely, a universal sense of the wrongness of existence, which (in conjunction with other more specific senses such as enunciated severally by great observers of the phenomena of religion like Schleiermacher and Otto) prepares the way for the manifestation of religion; (2) something wider and no less concrete than the religions, namely, the spheres of the spirit, which by their very nature are a step removed from conscious self-estimation as religions, which we should, however, prefer to treat as extensions of the religions or the families of religions. Even so, these spheres of the spirit will be tethered in our scheme to the religions or families of religions which alone constitute their self-identifying and self-preserving nuclei.

The differences between the religions can be examined in many ways, through doctrines, rituals, myths, approaches to salvation, etc. As a rule typological explanations are put to use in the service of these factors. Yet why the religions differ from one another in their essentials is a baffling question which those who seek to explain religion together with those who seek to explain it away must feel obliged, but also hard put to it, to answer. And no really satisfactory answer has yet been offered. Hegel is the chief among those who attempted to formulate one, in his case from the standpoints of the Spirit *(Geist)* and the Absolute religion, tracing the Spirit's journey through a well-chalked out path of progression including a complete route map of stages of development as well as stations of arrival and departure. But if we disregard this bold effort – and we must, as it can no longer put us under its constraint – we should be able to see that religions are unique entities containing at their core systems of revelation that refuse to be compared or subjected to grading or any kind of negotiations whatsoever. Even phenomenology must come to its terminus here, and it would be foolish to attempt a phenomenological account of revelation as such although such attempts are not wanting. But what can be subjected to phenomenological study is consciousness as it grasps these revelations and reshapes itself by jhem. If the opposite were the case, that is, if revelations were to be the ob-tects of comparison, the project of comparative study would, apart from failing to build any scientific foundation for itself, be promiting an act of irreverence repugnant to the self-interpretation of every great religion. Doc-trines, myths, symbols, rites – all those verbal and non-verbal expressions – must be considered the means by which consciousness grasps and reshapes itself by the revelations. Hence, naturally, they can be compared. But it is far better to go to the depths of awareness where these themselves took shape. Consciousness, therefore, continues to be that upon which we philo-sophically reflect.

At this point differences in types of consciousness must come to light. The type-determining factor governing consciousness must primarily be the revelations taken singly or collectively, with which each type has to do. But this can be said only provisionally, for, on the contrary, there abides the possibility that revelations, to the extent that they take up residence in consciousness cannot totally escape some reshaping in the process of their being grasped. Therefore, the mere discovery of correlation between types of consciousness and the respective revelations is the point beyond which phenomenology cannot hope to pass; and hence we must abandon all further consideration of causality relations as between the two or in any other way that affects each or both of them.

Here we must advert to term 'spheres of the spirit' (or 'spiritual spheres') which confessedly is not a happy choice, but there is none else equally serviceable by which to point to certain interrelated totalities or self-identical wholes – of moods, attitudes, orientations in thought, expressions in art, morality, etc., in fact all those items included in Hegel's *Phenomenology*. And yet, unlike Hegel, we must refrain from talking as though there were one single, unified, monolithic sphere, for the main reason that we do even-tually meet with different totalities or wholes distinguishable from one another. However, since we are committed to separating out two of these on the basis of our particular typological requirement, in the sense that they must represent polar elements, intersecting also with objective historical selectivity if possible, we are forced to limit ourselves to these in our explora-tion of 'the spheres of the spirit'. But there can take place a full dialogue between those two, which in fact would not only serve as model but act as nuc-leus for any larger enterprise in dialogue. Further, we must clarify that 'the spheres of the spirit' is not a discovery that has come about as the result of some metaphysical inquiry, which we totally by-pass, but of a very much more modest epistemological activity. There are many pointers to the existence of such spheres, which are what we start with in the same sense that in any comparative study of religion the awareness that different religions have different modes of existence is not the end product of one's search but rather the reason for beginning it. The objective of the study is to explore, briefly or extensively as the case may be, the horizons of the difference and also to ascertain if a mutual encompassing could be brought about.

Hence we start with facts that we encounter and nothing else, but in the process of inquiry we organize them by means of theoretical insights, as a consequence of which certain distinct spheres seem inexorably to come into view. In the quest for the nuclei around which everything crystallizes nothing would seem to fit so well as religions or families of religions, which however are regarded primarily for their historical identities rather than typological characteristics. 'The spheres of the spirit' as expressed by moods, attitudes, orientations in thought, art, etc., would seem clearly to persist even after, as is sometimes the case, the nuclei themselves may have reached the point of near-disintegration or have become all but invisible. It is true, strangely enough, that often some of the hidden potentialities of these nuclei reach a more powerful state of self-expression and realization only in movements that become consciously detached from, or reject, them or place themselves in a position of revolt against them. This seems to be particularly true of Christianity, which has a prodigious capacity to beget adversaries to itself, which however, might very well be an evidence of its super-normal powerfulness in shaping history.

Surely, it is impossible to understand the complete character of any of these nuclei unless we add to it the sum of all the movements that use it as reference point as well as point of departure. The interpretive integration of these various elements into each self-identifying nucleus is certainly one of the foremost tasks of the historian of each religion. Some historians of Christianity, who have received the Hegelian impetus, Ernst Troeltsch being probably the most luminous example, seem to have undertaken their work with this truth in mind. Accordingly, here singling out Christianity, it will be futile to endeavour to understand it without fully taking into account some of its profound self-expressions in its correlative sphere of the spirit, in thought, art and revolution. Rousseau, Kant, Hegel, Marx, Dostoevsky, Nietzsche and Heidegger are among the moderns who have brought Christianity to an incandescent state of self-expression in the Western sphere of the spirit. Modernity and all that goes with it, like technology, could have taken birth only in a sphere of the spirit where there has been a necessary openness towards time and therefore towards the future, and also towards space and therefore towards the universe, brought about at once by both a special kind of spiritual anxiety and the revolt against it as also by a reaction to physical and mental constrictions implicit in the myths of the cosmos. In contrast to the Western sphere of the Spirit, in the Indian one it is not so much revolutionary forms of thought as whole self-perpetuating and essentially timeless structures of knowledge and ritual action that continually express its self-identifying nucleus. Modernity with which it is faced today is not a growth from within but an essentially alien superimposition although it has enormous capacity to smoothly and perhaps passively adapt itself to modernity's external accidents. The invasion of anxiety structures is slower to be recognized or faced. This is true of the whole tranquillity-oriented sphere of the spirit.

BASIC DIFFERENCES BETWEEN ANXIETY-TYPE AND TRANQUILLITY-TYPE OF CONSCIOUSNESS

The words 'anxiety' and 'tranquillity' are here used to represent the two different types of consciousness expressed in two separate spheres of the spirit. In both cases the ultimate religious sources of insight have been decisive in shaping the consciousness. When we pass from the primeval forms of religion to the historic religions of revelation great events and great images loom large over the horizon, irrespective of whether such passage constitutes progress or regress. The sense of the wrongness of existence continues to call for symbolic and ritual structures of rectification, no doubt, but also call for much more: for radical new beginnings, what Walter Otto describes as renewal from the very roots.[2]

Anxiety can be detected as a fundamental element in Western spirituality, and indisputably it has its sources in Christianity itself as the Pauline writings above all will abundantly testify. It is related to the particular understanding of the cause of the world's predicament, but also to the end to which history moves. As St. Paul writes, 'for we know that the whole creation groaneth and travaileth in pain together until now. And not only *they* but ourselves also, which have the first fruits of the Spirit, even we ourselves groan within ourselves, waiting for the adoption, *to wit* the redemption of our body'.[3] The Christian expression of the spiritual life is definitely related to the *eschaton* and to its delay, to the expectation, anguish *and* relief involved in them. The particular expression of Christianity-determined Western consciousness is inalienable from this source.

In the Indian spiritual sphere determined by the Veda, Vedanta and Buddhism, whereas anxiety has always been recognized as the source of all human striving, most of all in religion, Reality begins where anxiety is terminated. It has been the belief that anxiety itself is the denial of Reality, since it is the character of the phenomenal world of becoming, to be both contained within its bounds, false as they are, and eventually burnt up along with that world. Anxiety must be totally forbidden to distort and pervert man's perception of Reality, which can mediate itself only in modes of tranquillity.

Now, obviously we cannot contend that all Indian religious and philosophical systems have the same view of Reality, for indeed the differences are vast. However, it is evident that the differences obtain at the metaphysical level or with reference to metaphysical questions, but by taking recourse to that possibility, achieved by modern phenomenological thought, of thinking ontology at the purely existential level, a divorce from questions of the former kind can be accomplished. In terms of existential ontology a reduction of otherwise diverse forms of Indian religious and philosophical traditions would seem possible. We can speak without exaggeration or distortion of what is common to Buddhism, Jainism and the various systems of Hindu religion. To put it simply, it concerns a state of being, of abiding, which transcends the anxiety-laden world of becoming. And that state is tranquillity. The Upaniṣadic seers, the Vedanta teachers, the *Mahābhārata*, the *Bhagavadgītā*, the Buddha and Mahāvīra are all basically agreed on this.

But an important fact may be pointed out. The Upaniṣads and even more obviously the Vedanta as a system hardly distinguished being from the state, that is, the state of awareness, and hence spoke of metaphysical and existential ontology in identical terms. But it is also true that every statement in the Upaniṣads that has the former connotation has also the latter. Clearly, in the Upaniṣads it is a state beyond all states being the Fourth *(turīyāvastha)* and it can be immanent in all others, a notion implicit in the very fact of our being able to speak about it. It is perceivable as a form of awareness and it constitutes the highest in all Indian religions as *kaivalya, prajñāpāramitā, bodha,* etc. Even for those who do not accept the Fourth *(turīya, caturtha)* as metaphysical Reality it is meaningful as a state of awareness from which, as the *Māṇḍūkya Upaniṣad* epitomizes through AUM, all meanings derive. It is described as tranquil, auspicious and non-dual *(śāntam, śivam, advaitam),* its essential sign being among other things, that it is signless *(alakṣana).*[4] This state is called the all-transcending abode *(sarvāparam dhāma),* characterized as tranquil, silent, fearless, sorrowless, blissful, contented, steadfast, immovable, undying, unshakable, enduring *(śāntam, aśabdam, abhayam, aśokam, ānandam, triptam, sthiram, acalam, amṛtam, acyutam, dhruvam).*[5]

Actually, the central Buddhist notion of Reality as the Void *(śūnya)* which, however, also signifies tranquillity and related properties can be derived from the Upaniṣads with stress on the transcendent state of awareness. The self that is in such a state is described by the *Maitrī Upaniṣad* in three places by the typical Buddhist word *śūnya* (void) along with the word *śānta* (tranquil) and other similar terms.[6] In fact in one of those places (II. 4) it is also described as *nirātma* (atmanless). The idea of tranquillity is conveyed not by the word *śānta* but also by the very word *nirvāṇa.*

Regardless of the controversy about the nature of metaphysical Reality – as between Buddhism and the Vedanta – there is no question but that thinking itself is required to be conducted in a spirit of tranquillity. Thus for instance the *Chāndogya Upaniṣad* says, 'verily all this is Brahman, from which all things arise, which sustains them (after they have arisen) and to which they return at dissolution; tranquil, one must meditate on it'.[7] One must cultivate tranquillity, for by the practice of Yoga one obtains it.[8]

Our own line of thought warrants us to consider only the existential properties of the tranquillity idea common to the Vedanta, Buddhism and indeed to all Indian (and by extension a whole universally prevalent type of) religious tradition, and we are not committed to any particular concept of Reality in respect of the traditional metaphysical debates. The controversies between Buddhism and the Vedanta have been among the most notable features of the history of Indian thought. We note this and pass on.

It is true, however, that Buddhism has laid itself wide open to a nihilistic interpretation of *śūnya* and *nirvāṇa*, its two leading concepts. When a whole line of modern interpreters argue that *śūnya* really means 'nothingness' and *nirvāṇa* 'extinction' they are not making any real innovation but simply repeating what orthodox Hindu critics have in sundry places and diverse manners said before. However, both the traditional Hindu and modern interpreters could be mistaken, the latter doubly so insofar as they may, like the former, have over-extended the meaning of the Buddhist texts or taken them too literally while failing to grasp the intent of the Hindu objectors. But this matter as far as we are concerned must rest here ensuring, however, openness towards that other strong current of scholarly Hindu opinion which has rejected the nihilistic estimate of the Buddhist doctrine.[9]

But it must be pointed out that while existential concern for tranquillity is present in equal degree in the Vedanta and Buddhism, the latter has gone about its philosophical business not only without commitment to any metaphysical view but without even interest in considering any, which is what is truly unique about it. Buddhism sought to bracket such inquiries and to divorce what to it appeared as the spurious metaphysical problem of being from a genuine existential ontology that has essentially to do with the state of tranquillity. Hence *nirvāṇa* remains, not by default, but by design, undefined. This implies that there is no warrant for characterizing *nirvāṇa* either as a state of being or as a state of non-being or as a state of being and non-being or as a state of neither being or non-being, which constitute the four speculative possibilities expressly shut out by the Buddha in visualizing the saint's condition after death. The last two alternatives are obviously absurd and could have neither logical nor empirical status as they can exist only in the pure abstraction of dialectical thought. One must infer, therefore, that the real intent in advancing this four-fold frame is to be neither metaphysical nor anti-metaphysical but to take a stand outside metaphysics altogether and to concentrate on an existential ontology which in this case is one of tranquillity. Functioning negatively and destructively, dialectics must be in the service of existential ontology. They must result in the abandonment of metaphysical inquiry. These sets of dialectical possibilities can also be reduced to a simple alternative as between *bhāva-dṛṣṭi* (view as existent) and *vibhāva-dṛṣṭi* (view as non-existent) and must be renounced. The Mādhyamika texts are even more explicit when it advocates the relinquishing of the consideration of *nirvāṇa* in terms of being and non-being *(bhāvābhava-parāmarśakṣayo nirvāṇam)*.[10]

Buddhism has been rightly considered the most difficult of all religions to interpret or to understand. Among the favourite over-simplifications are such clichés as, that it is essentially ethics, and that it is essentially psychology. Actually neither of these characterizations is correct. Tranquillity decidedly does not present a psychological perspective of Reality. If that were the case, then it deserves to be condemned in the same manner in which Heidegger has consigned *Dasein's* tranquillity *(Beruhigung)* to the realm of inauthenticity.[11] In recent years Buddhism has been, not incorrectly, described as an existential religion, but that description must be qualified by adding the condition that existentialism in this case is clearly one of tranquillity rather than of anxiety. As we have argued all along, the sense of the wrongness of existence is common to both spheres of the spirit and indeed to all of mankind's consciousness, and anxiety as sorrow *(duḥkha)* has been poignantly apprehended in Buddhism. But in Buddhism anxiety gives way to, and is resolved, in tranquillity which alone is thenceforth endowed with ontological dignity. What is true of Buddhism paramountly is equally true, although less conspicuously so perhaps, of other Indian religions. The true foundations of Indian religious perspectives are the tranquillity structures mediated through the teaching (*dharma* in Buddhism, and different *darśanas* in Hinduism); and the structures of suffering are placed as appendix to them, to be always seen from the tranquillity end like the upside down tree of the *Bhagavadgītā* with its roots above and branches below.[12] In the light of the tranquillity structures and in order the more deeply to enter into them the knowledge of the forms of sorrowfulness, in itself being of no value, may be acquired ritually or meditatively, assisted by catechetical and educational techniques of different kinds.

Now when we move to the threshold of the Western sphere we notice that anxiety has remained a most powerful idea, to show its great importance there having been one of the principal contributions of modern existentialist thought. In the light of this the current passage from the older metaphysics to new, existentially formulated ontologies has to be understood as a necessary self-expression of Western spirituality. Hence a thinker like Paul Tillich could write without embarrassment or apology that 'like finitude anxiety is an ontological quality'.[13] In fact, anxiety has remained an idea possessing the greatest ontological gravity and dignity. One of the most notable features of modern existentialist thought is that it has demonstrated vividly what has been implicit in the Western spiritual sphere, namely, the inseparability of the human self (for Heidegger *Dasein*) and anxiety and the rejection of alternatives.

Anxiety, it has been said by Kierkegaard 'must be viewed under the category of consciousness'.[14] And consciousness is not a phenomenon to be *suppressed* or *overcome* by means of the analytical knowledge of the chain of causation but an irreducible, unsublatable, untranslatable being whose existence is its essence, to be *understood* from within and without. Accordingly, it has to be perceived under the distinctive categories of will and relation.

Will is decisively important in this ontology. Kierkegaard expresses this whole approach to consciousness when he writes: 'The more consciousness the more will; the more will the more self. A man who has no will at all is no self; the more will he has the more consciousness of the self he has.'[15]

Relation like will is equally central. In certain modes it takes on the aspect of relation between the finite and the infinite. To quote Kierkegaard again: 'the self is the conscious synthesis of infinitude and finitude, which relates itself to itself, whose task is to become itself [a task to be accomplished only by means of relation to God.]'[16]

Now, when we move from religious existentialism to the existentialism that places itself outside religion, we notice a certain transposition. Thus in Heidegger's thought, the self-relating rather than God-relation becomes the real clue to the ontological possibility of *Dasein*, in fact in both its authentic and inauthentic modes.[17]

Certainly, in Christian thought and experience in particular and in the Western spiritual sphere as a whole, will [as also relation] is so dynamic and so central that rejection of it would amount to the rejection of the very problem of existence. In like manner the problem of relation (either as finite-infinite God-relation or pure self-relation) is also too vital to be disposed of by monistic arguments. These are both of the essence of Western ontology.

The dialectical character of infinitude-finitude relationship as it operates in consciousness provides one of the grounds for anxiety. Paul Tillich observes, 'finitude in awareness is anxiety'.[18] As none other than Heidegger points out (in *Vom Wesen des Grundes*), the concept of the world itself, so crucial in Western philosophy as well as in Christianity originated in the concept of this idea of relation as – here we use Versényi's language – 'at the very beginning of Western thought "world" really stood for a manner of being which was in some sense prior to all beings and was itself "relative to human *Dasein*".'[19] Heidegger's continuing exposition may be summarized again, in Versényi's words thus: 'Early Christian thought sharpened and reinforced this conception of the world to such an extent that in Paul and John "world" came to mean the mode of being of *Dasein* itself, the quality of being human as such in contrast to divinity, etc. ....'[20] The 'relational structure' to which the world belongs is presented as being characteristic of *Dasein* and accordingly we have good reason for surmising that if we fail to appreciate this we are apt to miss the real core of Western thought.

From there if we turn to the Hindu–Buddhist sphere we notice that, in contrast to the Western/Christian tradition, anxiety has been relegated to the realm of shadow-realities and hence refused ontological status. It can therefore be studied only in dispassion from the standpoint of its theoretical disappearance in tranquillity structures, hence from outside its own boundaries. It must always be seen together with other shadow-realities. As for relationship, so essential in the anxiety-based understanding of consciousness, the Vedanta simply consigns it to the unreal, as in its view essential consciousness is totally free of it, being unrelated even to itself. In that tradition consciousness *(cit)* is an own-sign *(svarūpalakṣaṇa)* of infinite Being and every conscious and finite-seeming being is called upon to recover its essential infinitude by realizing its absolute and irrelative identity with infinite Being. This perspective already establishes the indubitable possibility of tranquillity and every step thenceforth is to be nothing but a steady and calm actualization of it. Alternatively, as in Buddhism, the fore-knowledge of the unsubstantiability of consciousness (which is considered only as phenomenal) and the theoretical apprehension of the path of retracing the chain of becoming to (the Reality of) *śūnyata-nirvāṇa* accomplishes the same goal. Every form of anxiety or sorrow is a sign of a *seeming* alienation from Reality – in which in fact painfulness consists – and hence is without depth, because phenomena have no depth or substantiality. The theoretical perception of tranquillity will show up the shallow and unsubstantial character of sorrow: what has depth, reality, is the tranquillity state. And every man by hearing the revealed word of the Veda or the Buddha, or whatever the case, becomes transcendentally installed in that Reality, which, however, he must actualize in a serene and disciplined manner, preferably by the aid of one of the many forms of yoga.

THE GROUNDS OF DISTINCTION BETWEEN THE ANXIETY-TYPE AND THE TRANQUILLITY-TYPE

1. *Epistemological framework*

In order to perceive the primary category of existential ontology in each case we must have a knowledge of the epistemological framework in which it is bound. Let us take that of tranquillity first and see how the problem of sorrow is dealt with. The framework is the completed circle of Absolute Reality – Illusion (World) – Absolute Reality; the centre of thinking and of spiritual endeavour is Absolute Reality *(paramārtha satya)* which is the point where the circle begins as well as terminates. This point is known through *gnosis (vidyā, jnāna)* and there tranquillity reigns. Accordingly, as a man takes his stand on the Real he transcends sorrow and surveys it – when he does – as belonging to the world of illusion or at least of unsubstantial things and as no more calling for ontological examination. In the Western/ Christian sphere, on the contrary, the significance of the circle consists in its being never completed, which precisely is its existentiality. Undoubtedly, here too there must be an urge to return to the origin, which is clearly a universal demand. But as the anxiety-constituted and relational world is far from being unsubstantial, a simple return to, or recovery of, the origin is deemed impossible and as an act of inauthentic resignation. The world is frighteningly real and hence is not something that can be subtracted from Reality. Such seems to be its essential framework and although there are great variations in interpretation they are all variations within what is basically the same. One of the extremest interpretations come from the Exist-ential Movement itself, especially from Heidegger who strenuously argues for the belonging together of the world and *Dasein*. In the Christianity-determined spiritual sphere, anxiety is scrutinized with the eyes of anxiety and there exists the need to fathom its full depth through the manifold symbols of religion and culture as pre-condition to entertaining the possibility of tranquillity *per se*. The link between the reality of suffering and of the world and the Reality beyond them is established by a broken line, before which the whole tradition stops and which it ponders without ceasing. Faith, *pistis*, rather than *gnosis*, is that which arises in the pondering of the broken line representing the unbridgeable gap and the uncompleted circle. And faith is born in anxiety and bears the burden of uncertainty because the circle cannot be closed. Kierkegaard writes:

'The truth is precisely the venture which chooses an objective uncertainty with the passion of the infinite. I contemplate the order of nature in the hope of finding God, and I see omnipotence and wisdom and I also see much else that disturbs my mind and excites anxiety. The sum of all this is an objective uncertainty. But it is for this very reason that the inwardness becomes as intense as it is, for it embraces this objective uncertainty with the entire passion of the infinite .... But the above definition of truth is an equivalent expression for faith .... Faith is precisely the contradiction between the infinite passion of the individual's inwardness and the objective uncertainty.'[2]

The inexhaustible dynamo of faith thus oriented functions at its most powerful at the heart of Western religious tradition, by which increasingly with the passage of time, and not decreasingly, secular intellectuality itself seems to be charged. Thus the existentialists and Kant seem much more suffused with this spirit than the philosophers of earlier days. Assimilation of tranquillity structures such as emanated from old Western sources like Neo-platonism seem more and more out of tune with Western or modern actualities.

In the Indian tradition the paradigm treatment of the problem of suffering is to be found in the fundamental Four Noble Truths *(catvāri āryasatyāni)* of Buddhism, consisting of: (1) that there is suffering; (2) that there is a cause for it; (3) that there is a cure for it; (4) that the eight-fold path is the specific remedy. These four move in the manner of a circle and are perceived from the point of their completion. In the Western tradition, on the other hand, as the possibility of closing the circle is not entertained, the terminal existential point is where anxiety is infinitely intensified even if a leap over the gulf is visualized. Therefore, a truth that is left out of the completed circle of the Four Noble Truths, a fifth existential one, if we may so designate it in this context, becomes the focus for passionate concentration. And that concerns the dimension of meaning in the actuality of suffering, of anxiety, without attempting to point to a path out of its territory. The all-compelling character of this actuality can be witnessed most of all in its religious expression where God himself is represented as internalizing, Infinitizing and eternalizing it in a diversity of ways, particularly in the Incarnation. Here then, in thinking about existence there is a refusal to go beyond the boundary of the problematic; anxiety becomes not something to be overcome or resolved but something that must yield meaning.

2. *Existential orientation in the idea and the way of being*

The difference between the anxiety type and the tranquillity type of existential consciousness corresponds to a primeval difference in orientation in man's own being, both the idea and the way, to which the two divergent religious traditions give some clues. The division between polytheism and monotheism obviously is too formal to be consistently useful, but to begin with at least it furnishes us with some profound insights into this particular question of orientation. Wherever the unity of God has been stoutly maintained, man's being was apprehended as something given, the result of a gratuitous act on the part of a God who is not only Wholly Other but the true conferrer of being in every instance. Here a sheer feeling of gratuitousness clearly dominated as the conviction had been formed that the world had come into being for no reason at all but merely by virtue of the free act of a Creator who had willed it. What, however, is important here is not the theological dogma couched in which it usually comes but the way of conceiving all originated beings of which man sees himself as the self-conscious norm and measure. This way of conceiving existence is not just a self-stimulated intellectual act but rather the expression of a distinctive orientation implicit in man's perception of his own being and along with it all other beings; but it surely assumes also intellectual and conceptual modes.

This orientation in the idea and the way of being is attended by a unique ontological and religious attitude which may be best expressed by a word borrowed from the liturgy, 'doxology'. The Bible, particularly the Book of Psalms, gives expression to this better than any other text. The Creation story (or stories) in Genesis must be understood not so much in the light of an ordered account of events but in that of a doxological outburst, a singing of praise to God for the facts that man is and the world is, and above all, for the fact that God is. Here we see a truly doxological celebration of life under the condition of the oneness of God, who is creator. 'Make a joyful noise unto the Lord, all the earth; make a loud noise and rejoice and sing praise .... Let the sea roar and the fulness thereof; the world and they that dwell therein. Let the floods clap their hands; let the hills be joyful together,' so bids the Psalmist.[22] The words of St. Augustine have rung down the ages, appealing to men of devotion and men of thought alike, as he proclaimed, confessing:

"Great art thou O Lord, and greatly to be praised; great is thy power and infinite is thy wisdom." And man desires to praise thee, for he is part of thy creation; he bears his mortality about him and carries the evidence of his sin and the proof that thou dost resist the proud. Still he desires to praise thee, this man who is only a small part of thy creation. Thou hast prompted him that he should delight to praise thee, for thou hast made us for thyself and restless in our heart until it comes to thee.'[23]

It is not surprising that the Qur'an shares this doxological attitude which expresses man's view of his being in relation to God's sovereign will (though not to God's own being which is considered completely beyond human reckoning), in which the theme of praiseful human existence appears throughout. The most celebrated passage known by such titles as 'the opener' *(Al Fattah)*, 'the sura of praise, thanks and prayer', 'the mother of the book' etc. goes like this:[24]

> *Praise be to God. Lord of the world!*
> *The compassionate, the merciful!*
> *King of the day of reckoning!*
> *Thee only do we worship, and to thee only do we cry for help...*

Among the other striking passages is the following from the sura known as 'the prophets': 'All beings in heaven and earth are His: and they who are in His presence disdain not His service, neither are they wearied. They praise Him night and day and they rest not.'[25]

The religious attitude expressed in doxology had to do with much more than feeling, as it has behind it a distinct ontology. The joyfulness in being, however, is also vitiated by a profound sense of wrongness which consists in a primeval threat to the doxological existence, a threat that takes on the character of fallenness. Fallenness itself is the specific expression of the sense of wrongness that arises in this context; indeed it is the obverse side of gratuitousness. In biblical religion fallenness is the consequence of Fall, a primordial event which is to be interpreted as a deliberate and wilful act on the part of man, the effect of which is to add a negative condition to the positive condition of doxological existence. Nevertheless, it must be said that the divergences in theological and philosophical interpretation concerning fallenness, concerning the question of their correctness or otherwise, do not affect the fact that it is a distinctive idea to be set over against a completely different expression of wrongness found in the other sphere of the spirit. (In that other sphere there is no idea of fallenness; wrongness of existence is individuality itself, or in some few cases the mode of individuality).

This idea has in contemporary existentialist thought – in its non-religious expressions – been removed from its religious frame and expressed in what aims to be pure ontology. Heidegger himself had provided the strongest foundation for such efforts. In Heidegger's thought man's being appears as being thrown *(Geworfen)*, something that is disclosed to man as a matter in which he had had no choice. It simply amounts to saying that man's being is given to him. But this idea has been demythologized by Heidegger – by means of a transposition which has involved, vaguely, the following steps: (1) The addition of mood *(Stimmung)*[26] to the stuff of consciousness to be somehow juxtaposed with non-mood factors, of which we may regard the sense of the gratuitous givenness of being itself as primary. This has not involved total displacement of the latter. (2) The changing of gratuitousness into a matter of inherent constraint, made known through mood, in the sense that man realizes that 'he has to be', a fact apprehended as a project, a task to be accomplished in resoluteness,[27] rather than as a fact to look back to with wistfulness and fear.

Further, Heidegger considers man's being *(Dasein)* as fallen *(verfallen)*, which is explained as the falling away from itself as an authentic power to be its own self, into the 'world'.[28] Fallenness *(Verfallenheit)* is further described as absorption in being with one another *(Miteinandersein)* insofar as this being is led by prattle *(Gerede)*, curiosity *(Neugier)* and ambivalence *(Zweideutigkeit)*.[29] In Heidegger, then, the conversion from a religious to an extra-religious mould of the idea and way of being is thus complete; nevertheless it is a conversion of what was originally religious, in fact biblical. J. M. Robinson seems to be absolutely right in commenting: 'When one recalls that for Heidegger primal thinking is gratitude for the favour of being and thus becomes thanking, we may suspect that the Biblical analogy, rather than being a derivative of philosophic thought, is indeed the ultimate origin of Heidegger's insight. For here the thanksgiving emerges as the linguistic formulation of the reverent awareness that one's being is God's creation.'[30]

Falleness is exactly the point at which religion in the Western sphere begins its upward struggle; it is also the point of beginning for Christianity-inspired Western civilization and history. In the light of this fact Eliade's concluding sentence in *Cosmos and History* is full of truth. 'In this respect', he writes, 'Christianity incontestably proves to be the religion of 'fallen man', and this to the extent to which modern man is irredeemably identified with history and progress....'[31] Incidentally speaking, anxiety centred in the awareness of fallenness seems to have furnished the motives for modernity, ideology and technology (all of which are inseparable from one another, a point well expressed by Heidegger in several of his writings).[32] Such projects involve 'the will to will' elimination of 'the fate-ladenness of existence' owing to 'the initiative of being pressing in upon thought'.[33] It is undoubtedly true that only Christianity could have created the mental and spiritual climate necessary for these things to arise.

In polytheistic religious views, man's being is not thought of as gratuitous givenness but as fortuitous occurrence. Ontologically, the gods have the same status as men and they are all governed by the same transcendent law of the cosmos as is supremely exemplified in the *Ṛta* idea of the *Ṛgveda*; the only difference is that insofar as the gods in their inner essence have an identity with the supreme law (as Indra, Varuṇa and some of the other gods are called *Ṛtavan*, as they are possessors of *Ṛta*), they hold superintendence over man's conduct as well as over the working of the universe.

In Vedic and subsequent stages of Hindu religion man is placed in many situations of worship to the gods or to one supreme God, indifferently, and while all manner of fervent gratitude for favours received is expressed, the sense of ontological indebtedness to the gods for man's own being, repayable or otherwise, is conspicuously lacking, because being is the result of no one's favour; likewise among the various forms of supplication, in spite of some seeming exceptions to the rule, found in the *Bhakti* (devotional) literature there is none that has any clear ontological bearing. No doubt an interlocutor could object by calling attention to the vast *stuti* (adulatory) literature and more specifically to the *Sahasranāma Stotras* in the *Mahābhārata* and the eighteen *purānas* which are the ritual recitation of the thousand names of Devi, Viṣṇu or Śiva as the case may be. The closest that we can come to even in the *Viṣṇu Sahasranāma* (Thousand names of *Viṣṇu*) in the *Mahābhārata*, which is the greatest of these, are the two adjectives of God, *Bhūtābhrt* (sustainer of beings) and *Bhūtabhāvanah* (the poetic arranger of beings).[34] (In fact Śankara one of those who comment on the work takes pains to point out that praise is an ontologically meaningless form of statement.)[35] Even in Rāmānuja the sense of gratuitous givenness does not exist. The *Dhammapāda* is quite unequivocal when it says, *attā (ātmā) attano natho, attā hi attano gatih* (the self alone is its owner, the self alone is its redemption).[36] Through ecstasy, trance *(samādhi)*, through unitive knowledge, every one may reach the transcendent state surpassing the fortuitousness of individual being. Such is everyone's destiny. Surely the prospect of an ecstatic apprehension of the divine originally mediated in polytheism could take two contrary tacks.

With respect to Greece we are told by such a competent authority as Walter Otto that while 'Homeric poems are filled with divine proximity and presence', the visage of the divine was displayed in nature itself.[37] However, although one may gather here the impression of the rightness of existence in an ecstatic harmony with nature as reflected by the gods, as Walter Otto points out, such is far from being the case. To quote Otto: 'The Darkest Sphere of life yet remains, and if here too the gods are encountered they would themselves seem to contradict the impression of brightness which they have communicated to us.' 'How is it possible,' he immediately asks, 'that the geniuses of life, abundance and fortune should likewise be the source of distress, doom and destruction?'[38] The solution is found in the idea of fate *(Moira)*. Now, although sometimes, 'it may appear that the decree of fate allots some positive good to man', 'from the totality of its functions there can be no doubt that its character is not positive but negative'.[39] 'Death itself is the prime meaning of fate.'[40] Explaining this Walter Otto writes: 'This idea points to two realms, which are alien to one another: a realm of life, of development, of affirmation, and a realm of death, severance and denial. Only the former is configured, active, personal; the realm of negation has neither figure nor personality; it only sets limits and with its cry of Halt! sharply curtails development and life. On this the gods have no more to say. They serve the consummation of fate but only in the degree that the full and protected life must serve the fall of a life that is lost and is without protection.'[41]

Fate, then, seems to be a way of adjusting the fortuitousness of man's being to the sense of the wrongness of existence, with the rightness of nature as a backdrop. In this context one may make a reference to the importance of ecstasy as a category of apprehension of being that prevailed in some forms of ancient religion and philosophy, appearing again in contemporary phenomenological thought, but any further treatment of it has to be forbidden here as its many ramifications would go beyond the range of this essay.[42]

Vedic polytheism in spite of its affinities with Greek religion particularly in respect of the rightness of nature and the manifestation of the gods but without any definite notion of fate, has eventually worked towards transcending nature with the climax ultimately reached in the Upaniṣads from where it was continued by various philosophical movements. *Samādhi*, ecstasy, became the generic means of returning fortuitous existence to Ultimate Reality. In order to accomplish this, one must know the source from which all beings come, for as the *Bṛhadāraṇyaka Upaniṣad* says, 'As a spider moves along the thread, as sparks come from the fire, even so from the Self come forth all breaths, all worlds, all divinities, all beings. Its mystery is the truth of truth *(satyasya satyam)*. Vital breaths are the truth and their truth is it (Self).'[43] Gradually this fortuitous coming into being was explained as due to the subtle mechanism of *karma-samsāra*, which is not a single, primordial event but a series of self-positing acts *(karmas)* in terms of which man must understand his own existence. The phenomenon called individuality comes about fortuitously as a consequence of *karma*. Therefore, as the *Gītā* says, 'men who are united with wisdom *(budhiyuktāh)*, relinquishing the fruits of *karma* and freed from the bonds of birth go to where there is no evil *(anāmayam)*'.[44] The Indian accounts of the wrongness of existence and its solutions are radical. Phenomenality and attachment to it themselves constitute the wrongness, not just some aspect of it, nor any after-event. There is no mystery here which the gods may know better than men. In fact the gods as cosmic powers and symbols, whom men continue to adore and worship for courtesy or temporal or meditational benefit, do only obscure the face of truth. One may invoke them just so that they may help to unconceal what they have concealed by reason of the role they play in man's psychology of perception as it is said in the *Īśā Upaniṣad*: 'The face of truth is covered with a golden disc: Unveil it, O! Puṣan so that the lover of truth may see it *(satyadharmāya dṛṣṭaye)*.'[45] The inherent thrust of polytheism has been to transcend itself, which was accomplished as early as the Upaniṣads. Therefore, man's being, fortuitous as it is, has nothing further essentially to do with the gods; its wrongness has been fully accounted for, and the way to its overcoming also well established, with details varying according to the particular systems.

3. *Existential orientation towards the Absent*

Finally, in looking for the grounds of differentiation between the two types of consciousness we must pay attention to the problem of existential orientation towards the Absent. Even the statement 'God does not exist' must be interpreted in different ways according to the spheres of the spirit.

In the Judeao-Christian context such a statement as the above can only mean the concrete non-existence of a particular Who-God who dwells in the expectation of the people concerned but mysteriously fails to fulfill the expectation. The trauma of the Hebrew prophetic consciousness and more especially in Job seems essentially to consist in this. In a sense the theology of the Death of God is a very telling although caricatured and perhaps commercialized expression of this point. The celebrated atheisms of Nietzsche and Sartre openly concern the non-existence of a Who-God thus conceived. These are existential applications of a *particular* Non-Being, projected as a *non-existent* God. Such applications must always have a difinite bearing on the active character of Reality and must always have a focus in history and the realm of human social existence and hence must become ideological, and may take on, occasionally, extreme nihilistic forms.[46]

Such nihilisms have a special but indubitable religious character, being based on a special sense of the Absent Divine and therefore being a profound expression of anxiety. Kierkegaard brings to bear one of his deepest insights when he writes, quite relevantly to this issue, 'Suppose Christianity is subjectivity, an inner transformation, an actualization of inwardness, and that only two kinds of people can know anything about it; those with an infinite passionate happiness base their happiness upon a believing relationship to Christianity, and those with an opposite passion, but in passion reject it – the happy and the unhappy lovers.'[47] The story of anxiety in the Western sphere of the spirit is perfectly expressed here. There has undoubtedly been a bifurcation but Christianly conceived transcendence surely remains the common point of reference. As Karl Jaspers points out, Dostoevsky, Kierkegaard and many others, are in the former category, while Nietzsche and also some others are obviously in the latter. 'Nietzsche's leap to doctrines,' in Jasper's interpretation, is not a leap to tradition (as in Dostoevsky and Kierkegaard) but to self-made beliefs and self-devised symbols – superman, eternal recurrence, Dionysius, etc., – that are wholly lacking in historically convincing atmosphere.[48] Whether Jaspers is right or wrong in this pronouncement with regard to Nietzsche particularly is not important, the real point being that: (1) anxiety is used as a means to reach the source from which it came; (2) for doing so two contrary paths can be followed. However, in the one path anxiety inevitably remains and is intensified through the knowledge of the source; while in the other the knowledge of the source is allowed only a hidden, rather than open, existence and for that very reason it is made much more poignant. Here Jaspers seems to be right, as he observes: 'Nietzsche expressed godlessness in a manner that conveys his unspeakable torment: Having to renouce God means that you will never again pray ... never again find peace in boundless trust; you deny yourself the opportunity to come to rest before a final wisdom, final goodness.'[49]

Over against this above type of the Absent Divine, the famed theory of the Void *(śūnya-vāda)* in Buddhism is to be understood as really a religious theory of *universal* Non-Being with no reference to history or expectation or activity, and hence as absolutely different from the Western views of nothingness and Western types of atheism. Nothingness conceived thus has its own reference point, which is the Vedantic doctrine of *universal* Being, Brahman.

Now as to whether *Śūnyatā* of the idealistic schools of Buddhism should be regarded as sheer nothingness or not will be answered by this. But the controversy between orthodox Hindu systems and Buddhist dialectical schools as to the metaphysical implications of this doctrine is of no consequence as far as our inquiry is concerned. However, that the Hindu characterizations of it in a purely negative manner may be wrong is recognized by an increasing number of eminent scholars.[50] Regardless of the merits of the case on either side of the controversy the simple phenomenological facts are: (1) *Śūnyatā* of Buddhism is indeed the radicalization of the Vedantic theory of Being (Brahman) to which parts of the Upaniṣads themselves lead the way; (2) it is the object of intense religious striving and constitutes 'Reality' and is the source of tranquillity.

In all Indian religions the true destiny of phenomenal consciousness to which it must be directed by the sternest of disciplines possible, by the methods of mental and spiritual concentration, is to negate itself as well as all name-form *(nāma-rūpa)* phenomena as such so that the potentiality for Reality can be recovered in the tranquillity of non-becoming, irrespective of whether Reality is to be conceived as pure Universal Being or pure Universal Non-Being. Somehow at the level of Reality itself the difference between Being and Non-Being would seem to wither away. And tranquillity, in which Reality is realized and by means of which it manifests itself to all seekers, mut not be considered as conditioned psyche but unconditioned knowledge, gnosis. Reality is achieved by reversing the processes of the phenomena of becoming not to the point of the ultimate potentiality for becoming but to the point beyond. The man of the spirit has in principle already reached it, for not to think tranquillity and non-becoming is to deny his spiritual destiny and the true nature of his striving. From that point his 'relation' to phenomena is no more than authentic expression of essential non-relation and hence wholly averse to any anxiety possibility. But in this manner it is evident that it chooses to regard anxiety only as the sum of the modes of individual psyche and closes itself to the unfathomable depth of anxiety which for the other sphere of the spirit is a key to Reality and ought not to be lost or thrown away. A glance in the opposite direction, that is, towards the key of tranquillity, it seems, it is necessary also to cast.

Finally, it needs to be reiterated that what are being talked about in terms of anxiety and tranquillity are only the comprehensible essences of the religions expressed in the respective spiritual spheres, which alone we can compare. As for the incomprehensible essences of the religions, their essential revelations, which the spiritual spheres themselves may not fully embody, we must always be in search of them and cannot hope to have reached them. But the light furnished by the spiritual spheres are indispensable, however faltering our steps. For without lying about Reality, they and they alone provide us with the means of self-knowing.

8

Anxiety and Tranquillity: Some Associated Notions

TWO TYPES OF INWARDNESS

As we move further along the two parallel roads of the spiritual life signified by the terms 'anxiety' and 'tranquillity' the conviction is deepened in us that we are dealing with two different types of inwardness also: anxiety inwardness is one and tranquillity inwardness another. The superficial efforts on the part of many who are thought-weary to proffer the philosophy of tranquillity as *answer* to the problems of anxiety must be deemed to have arisen from some profound misunderstanding. This misunderstanding is rooted in thinking anxiety and tranquillity to be psychological, which is decidedly not the case. Again, the method often followed by many writers in the field of Eastern and comparative idealism and mysticism of relegating anxiety to the realm of the object or the outward on the one hand and to finitude on the other, while elevating tranquillity to the region of pure subject and inward reality must be abandoned as misleading and worthless.

Anxiety is a genuine form of subjectivity or inwardness, although surely not the only one. Besides, it must be realised that it has infinite depth itself and it is not the case, as many imagine, that it is only shallowness whereas tranquillity is depth. As Kierkegaard writes: 'The religious posits decisively an opposition between the outward and the inward, posits it decisively as opposition between the outward and the inward, and therein lies suffering as an existence-category for the religious life, but therein lies also the inner infinity of inwardness inwardly directed.'[1] Kierkegaard is the truly representative thinker of the Christian West to fathom the depth of inwardness in anxiety and to give it eloquent expression (although sometimes in a rather forced manner). He is quite right in viewing anxiety and faith as counterparts to each other in respect of inwardness so that the depth of the one could meet the depth of the other. He depicted faith as the taking of risk in a situation where objective knowledge is not possible. And faith therefore is passion. In Kierkegaard's words, '[For] without risk, there is no faith, and the greater the risk the greater the faith; the more objective security the less inwardness (for inwardness is precisely subjectivity), and the less objective security the more profound the possible inwardness.'[2] The uncertainty of Socratic philosophy is intensified in Christian faith, which means that 'the Socratic existential inwardness is as Greek light-mindedness in comparison with the grave strenuosity of faith'.[3]

In keeping with our pattern of division it is recognized that the tranquillity type of inwardness occurs in another sphere of the spirit, and it is Indian religious philosophy that expresses it pre-eminently. This latter type consists in achieving formal disconnection from all structures of becoming through the greater inwardization of one's own essence through one of the several alternative forms of gnosis, such as *vidyā* (the Vedanta), *viveka-jñāna* (Sānkhya-yoga), *kevalajnāna* (Jainism), *prajñā* (Buddhism) etc. It can only be accomplished by being devoid of all passion. It would not be necessary to expand this theme as it is so basic in all Indian religious and philosophical systems; all that is needed is what is being done here, namely, to expose each type of inwardness to the light of the other. Now we must outline a few associated notions assignable to these different types of inwardness.

CONSCIENCE AND GUILT

Between the inwardness of anxiety and conscience there is an undeniable connection. Tillich calls attention to the fact that Nietzsche, who not only thought anxiety but lived it more poignantly than any other modern that we know of (with the probable exception of Dostoevsky and Kafka) had asserted this connection. Tillich observes: 'Even Nietzsche who attacks more passionately than anyone else, the judging conscience, derives the birth of the 'inner man' from its appearance.'[4] Conscience undoubtedly accompanied the birth of tragedy. There is, of course, no debate about the question that as a fact of human consciousness, conscience is universal. However the *concept* of conscience *(syneidesis)*, philosophically a creation of the Greeks, underwent a revaluation in Christian thought on account of the link with sin and guilt. We are forced to distinguish between conscience as a notion and fact of general morality, whose incidence as such is universal, and conscience as an ontological idea having something positively to say about man. In its sociological genesis, it may be reasonably asserted, as has often been, that insofar as it is associated with the rise of individuality it could have come about only as a result of the breakdown of the we-consciousness of primitive conformism.[5]

Although in the later prophetic writings of the Old Testament the link between conscience and individual self-hood with the idea of a God before whom one stands in judgment is apparent, it is St. Paul who fashioned conscience as a category of self-knowledge in the service of religious thought. St. Paul writes: 'For when the Gentiles, which have not the law, do by nature the things contained in the law, these, having not the law, are a law unto themselves: Which show the work of the law written in their hearts, their conscience also bearing witness, and *their* thoughts the mean while accusing or else excusing one another.'[6] However, Tillich's dictum that in the New Testament, conscience 'has religious significance only indirectly', being 'primarily an ethical category', an element of human nature generally, 'to be called into action as the instrument of accusation and condemnation in the context of the non-fulfilment of the law. . .' may be conceded purely from a historical and theological-exegetical point of view, for the fact remains that in it has been planted the seeds of a most vital ontological revaluation of man to germinate and to grow in course of time.

Conscience, as scholars know, played a great role in Medieval and a greater role in Reformation religious thought. Again, through the instrumentality of Kant and Ritschl it became a very active notion in modern Western theology. It was formally introduced into philosophy and ethics by Butler who made it a central problem in ethical theory.[7] It has had the greatest vogue in the thought of Hobbes, Hume, Shaftesbury, Thomas Reid, Kant, Hegel, Nietzsche and Heidegger. Kant subjects it to the most penetrating analysis of all. He writes, 'Every man has a conscience, and finds himself observed by an inward judge which threatens and keeps him in awe . . . which is incorporated in his being.'[8] He emerges with the conclusion that conscience is the consciousness of the 'categorical imperative' and yet as consciousness it is itself a duty.

Hegel's thought on conscience has to be traced through the tortuous pathways of his system. A basic principle is that 'conscience is the self which knows and wills'.[9] Hegel stipulates, in a way revising Kant, 'Conscience, then, in its majestic sublimity above any specific law and every content of duty, puts whatever content it pleases into its knowledge and willing.'[10] Conscience is elevated to the highest level as it is described as the self, contemplating its own 'proper divinity', as 'pure inward self-knowledge' and hence as constituting a 'solitary worship', 'Service of God', etc.[11] Hegel wants to push conscience beyond morality and the polarities associated with it. In fact, his inquiry into this question arose from a desire to resolve 'the antimonies in the moral view of the world – viz., that there is a moral view and that there is none'.[12]

The West has had to deal with conscience as an existential problem, given the anxiety structure of consciousness of which it is an associate. Even the tendency to reach out to a transmoral conscience, surely from the anxiety frame in which it has been held and grown, is an expression of this necessity. What comes to the fore is a conscience about conscience, that is, conscience's own infinite reflexiveness, and anguished awareness of its being there as the goad against which one kicks – and irremovable, try as hard as one might. Its presence and witness in practical morality could of course be far more easily tolerated than the fact of its being there like a boulder in the foreground of man's self-perception. It would appear that while morally it is bearable, ontologically it is not.

The anguish of having conscience, kept under the restraint of duty in Kant and temporarily transformed into the freedom of transmoral self-determination in Hegel, broke loose and became a painful cry in Nietzsche. So this conscience about conscience, this anguish, took on in Nietzsche's thought the form of 'bad conscience', which he nevertheless felt to be the source of good as he explains, 'the bad conscience is a sickness but it is a sickness as pregnancy is one'.[13] Bad conscience is also the source of creativity in history, literature, art and philosophy. As Tillich interprets it, 'it gives evidence to the assertion that the uneasy, accusing and judging conscience is the original phenomenon; that the good conscience is only the absence of the bad conscience; that the demanding and warning conscience is only the anticipation of it'.[14]

This particular thrust in the problem of conscience assumes the greatest gravity in Heidegger and the anguished, ejaculatory, primal utterances of Nietzsche are replaced by more seemingly placid existential-ontological analysis.[15] Nevertheless, beneath the surface calm the agony is unmistakably there. Conscience has been described as a call, the call of care. Specifically, it is *Dasein* calling itself.[16] Although both the Caller and the Called are one and the same an ontological distinction is to be made, the reason being, put in the form of the question: 'When *Dasein is* appealed to *is* it not there in a different way from that in which it does the Calling', although we might say that the call which is *Dasein's* 'ownmost potentiality-for-Being functions as the caller'?[17] Also the unexpected and involuntary character of the call is what makes it an objective 'It'. 'Indeed,' says Heidegger, 'the call is precisely something which we ourselves have neither planned nor prepared for nor voluntarily performed nor have even done so. "It" calls against our expectations and even against our will. On the other hand, the call undoubtedly does not come from someone else who is with me in the world. The call comes from me and yet *from beyond me*.'[18]

The relation between conscience and anxiety is made obvious. We are told that in the face of 'nothingness' what faces *Dasein* 'is anxious with anxiety about its ownmost potentiality-for-Being'. With respect to the link between the two, the inescapable impression created is that anxiety does include anxiety about having a conscience insofar as it does look for an accounting of its origin in the depth of *Dasein's* uncanniness. So then, 'what if this *Dasein*, which finds itself in the very depth of its uncanniness, should be the caller of the call of conscience'.[19] It would appear that even the urge to arrive at a transmoral conscience manifested in Hegel, Nietzsche and some others (like Giordano Bruno) in different ways is the result of wanting to reach a reality from where one can freely determine the good without the constraint of law or duty. Hegel, accordingly, expressed the principle that conscience 'determines from itself alone' but added to it the principle of 'sensibility' which is none other than the 'circle of the self within which determination as such falls'.[20] Therefore he said, 'it is now the law which exist for the sake of the self and not the law for the sake of which the self exists'.[21]

It is clear that in all these philosophers conscience pertains not so much to the isolated realm of ethics as to the existential dimensions of ontology. In all of them conscience about conscience is the pervasive problem. In this context an observation made by Tillich is quite pertinent. He writes, 'A transmoral conscience does not deny the moral realm, but it is driven beyond it by the unbearable tensions of the moral law.'[22] The real pathos comes from the fact that conscience which makes necessary the choosing of all actions in resoluteness is itself not a matter of choice. Thus self-determining freedom is seen to come to its limit unless one takes the less profound alternative offered by Sartre, namely the exultation in a fancied freedom of unfreedom.

Conscience has always gone with guilt. Shakespeare puts the following immortal words on the tongue of Richard III:[23]

> *My conscience hath a thousand several tongues,*
> *And every tongue brings a several tale,*
> *And every tale condemns me for a villain.*
> *Perjury, perjury, in the highest degree;*
> *Murder, stern murder in the dir'st degree,*
> *All several sins, all us'd in each degree,*
> *Throng to the bar, crying all, Guilty! Guilty!*
> *I shall despair.*

But in conscience about conscience the association with guilt is very deep-rooted. Christianity has understood guilt as a fact that results from – and causes – sinning, which is 'falling short of the glory of God', in other words the primary modality of the negative condition of the Fall that has vitiated the doxological way of being. Philosophically speaking, it must be construed as a teleological matter implying a distance between the actuality and the lost but regainable possibility in human existence. Tillich illuminates the problem as he suggests that 'since the self discovers itself in the experience of a split between what it is and what it ought to be, the basic character of conscience – the consciousness of guilt is obvious'.[24]

Hegel demonstrates the unavoidability of guilt as it is internal to the act and the act internal to the self. To quote him: 'Guilt is not an external indifferent entity *(Wesen)* with the double meaning, that the deed as actuality manifested to the light of day, may be an action of the guilty self, or may not be so, as if with the doing of it there could be connected something external and accidental that did not belong to it, from which point of view therefore, the action could be innocent.'[25]

Heidegger pushes the connection between conscience and guilt even further, and there is no better clue to the understanding of his ideas about it than the category of conscience concerning conscience. Thus among other ways it is expressed as the problem of *wanting to have a conscience (Gewissen-haben-wollen)*. For observe:

'In understanding the call, *Dasein* lets its inmost Self *take actions in itself (in sich handlen)* in terms of that potentiality-for-Being which it has chosen only so that it can *be* answerable *(verantwortlich)*. Factically, however, any taking action is necessarily 'conscienceless', not only because it may fail to avoid some factical moral indebtedness, but because on the null basis of its null projection, it has, in Being with Others, already become guilty towards them. Thus one's wanting-to-have-a-conscience becomes the taking-over of that essential consciencelessness within which alone the existentiell possibility of *being* 'good' subsists.'[26]

Heidegger informs us also that 'being guilty is more primordial than any knowledge of it', that '*Dasein* is guilty in the basis of its Being', because of which alone 'is conscience possible'.[27] All this amounts to a verdict that guilt is the father of conscience in the specific form nurtured in the Western/ Christian sphere of the spirit. The existentialist doctrine of conscience, arising from the knowledge of that mysterious phenomenon turning upon itself, could not but take on the involved and reflexive aspect, though nowhere explicitly stated so, of conscience about the fact that there is conscience, and could not have developed except by exploiting the more fully the profound ontological implications of guilt which is so central an idea in Christianity.

THE COUNTERPART OF CONSCIENCE AND GUILT IN THE TRANQUILLITY SPHERE

As has been observed before, conscience as such is a universal phenomenon and is present in all human beings irrespective of spheres of the spirit. Likewise morals and ethical thought are also undeniably universal. However, what is unique about the anxiety sphere, as has been made clear, is the anguished concern about the fact of conscience.

The tranquillity sphere, as already demonstrated at length, is pre-eminently represented by the Indian religions. Here it is well known that it is Buddhism that has had a commonly acknowledged ethical character. Yet even there we note the significant absence of reflection on conscience. The closest that we can come to such a reflection in the religious systems of India is in the

Pūrva-mīmāṁsā. But there, as one outstanding scholar, S. K. Maitra, quite correctly observes, 'the analysis of conscience or consciousness of duty (as in nearly all Hindu systems) [thus] resolves itself into the analysis of the consciousness of authority which is attached to a scriptural imperative or prescription'.[28]

Conscience as the power of discrimination in ordinary moral conduct, that is, between good and evil, right and wrong, truth and untruth, violence and non-violence, is surely assumed to be resident in consciousness. Hence the four fundamental moral norms, *satya* (truthfulness), *āsteya* (non-covetousness), *aparigraha* (non-appropriation) and *ahiṁsā* (non-violence) which are inculcated in all branches of Indian religions, whether Hindu, Buddhist or Jaina. But these are pure precepts which, it is taken for granted, are within man's competence to practice. Except for providing the impulsion to practice them to the letter, conscience plays no further role and certainly not that of an accusing, judging and condemning power towards those who fail to obey these noble precepts. But the *Pūrva-mīmāṁsā*, which engages in reflection upon conscience leads the way in formalizing the phenomenon under a system of scriptural injunctions or commands *(vidhi)* into which the whole ethical code has been forced. Thus all categories of morals are either replaced or completed by that of duty, ceremonial as well as other, made known through Vedic injunctions, which generates in the individual a special kind of conscience or consciousness of duty, called *vidhipratyaya*.

We note the existence of two main streams of interpretation in the *Pūrva-mīmāṁsā* as to how conscience operates, and both are no doubt formal. The Bhaṭṭas advance the theory of two *bhāvanas* (expressions), that of the word *(śabda)* and that of meaning or actualization *(artha)*. Maitra explains: 'Thus one becomes conscious of a *śabda-bhāvana* or operative process of the imperative when one hears a scriptural injunction and one is also conscious of an *artha-bhāvana* or process of becoming in the self through which the imperative is realized in action.'[29] The other stream represented by the Prabhākaras reject the theory of the two *bhāvanas* and argue that the scriptural command is realized through a unique mode of consciousness called *ātmakūṭa*, meaning an impulsion to the moral will in the self.[30] It has been customary to translate *ātmakūṭa* by 'conscience'. It has been defined as a unique and unanalysable feeling although probably not *sui generis* as it is generated or at least awakened by the scriptural word. The ramifications of the differences between these two streams are very great, as the first implies a degree of inward determination imposed by the hearing of the law whereas the other only illuminates and creates motives in consciousness. In either case the operation of 'conscience' is limited to obeying the law and does not govern the internal consequences of disobedience in freedom.

Karma-saṁsāra or the cycle of rebirth conditional on acts is not, in the *Pūrva-mīmāṁsā,* or any other intepretation, an expression of internal consequence because the chain of becoming – birth, death and rebirth – is an externalized order contingent upon acts and their fruits, which can be lived out and endured in indefinite extension, and consequently the life subjected to it can be redeemed by wisdom (gnosis), control of motives and self-discipline. By contrast, the problem of disobedience of the law, strangely enough unavoidable – not in spite of but because of freedom – is lodged in the very heart of the Christian version of conscience. And for this reason conscience had to be taken up into the ontology of human existence itself in a way that bears no parallel in any of the religions of the East. On account of this it is clear that only in Christianity does conscience have its source in guilt which is not true of the Eastern religions – or any other for that matter.

In the light of freedom causality has no meaning although causes are assigned as a way of speaking and as a way of thinking. It is necessary that causality be assimilated into paradox, for to man's condition of fallenness and to his guiltiness no non-paradoxical cause can be assigned, which means that a cause is that which makes the unnecessary necessary just so that existence itself be possible. Causality therefore in the anxiety sphere must be associated with responsibility in freedom and as such can only intensify the anguish of conscience as it has to be held accountable for what it cannot be held accountable for. On the contrary, *karma-saṁsāra* is causality pure and simple, operating with predictable, mechanistic regularity and uniformity of motion, with no implication of paradox that the individual may be aware of.

Karma-saṁsāra is predicated on the becoming character of phenomenal consciousness upon the cessation of which one must concentrate as an expression of one's realized inwardness for the sake of ultimate release from sorrow, in other words, phenomenality itself. While undoubtedly, conscience itself is a fact of everyday life as well as of specialized and formalized ethicoceremonial life of obedience to the revealed word, there is no such a thing as conscience about conscience in the Indian sphere of spirituality. The object of anguished concern is not conscience but the fact of phenomenal consciousness upon which *karma-saṁsāra* rests; but then the concern is essentially negative in the sense that one's primary obligation to oneself is to seek to put an end to it or to break its cycle for oneself. One puts an end to it or breaks its cycle by means of a proportionally modulated replacement of the concern about the becoming consciousness, the real villain of the piece, with gnosis.

The secret of gnosis consists in becoming aware of the true nature of *karma-saṁsāra* itself. *Karma-saṁsāra* is mere externality; it is perceived as a causal mechanism that does not affect the inward reality of man. Hence it generates no notion of guiltiness. Essentially man remains always innocent. The striving of *dharma* is to embody innocence in the domains of life and to enable man to act with deliberate innocence. Here it must be observed that Kierkegaard's exposition of innocence as ignorance which may at most create a purely psychological kind of dread, set up in contrast with guilt (which is knowledge, no doubt) where the dread is existential (and therefore profound),[31] clearly does not fit our case, for *dharma* is deliberate and gnostic (not ignorant) innocence from which at any time a 'qualitative leap' or a dialectical transition to guilt, as Kierkegaard provides for, would be impossible. Hence it has to be declared that it belongs to another sphere of the spirit of which Kierkegaard had no knowledge. But obviously he was speaking theologically, from a Christian standpoint, about a kind of innocence outside Christianity which Christianity is bound to dialectically absorb. But such absorbtion, however dialectically contrived, is not possible vis-à-vis *dharma*. *Dharma*-innocence is not considered a protection against guilt, which in any case does not arise, but against the threat of the strengthening of the bondage that the continuance of the chain of *karma-samsāra* betokens. This particular freedom motif is expressed in the doctrine of desireless action *(niṣkāma-karma)*, classically spelt out in the *Bhagavadgītā*. By becoming a *yukta* (united one) a person avoids the prospect of becoming a *baddha* (bound one).

> The *yukta* (united one) attains to tranquillity
>   By abandoning the fruits of action;

But the *ayukta* (ununited one) is impelled by desire
  And by being attached to fruits (of action) is bound.[32]
Action is said to be the means of the sage
  Who wishes to attain to yoga (union);
When he has achieved yoga
  Serenity is said to be the means.[33]

It is necessary to contrast the Indian view with the Western with respect to guilt; in order to do so in this context Hegel's clarification will be of immense value. Ruling out the possibility that any action could be innocent, he declares: 'Rather the action itself is this diremption, the affirming itself for itself, and establishing over against this an alien external reality. That such a reality exists is due to the deed itself, and is the outcome of it. Hence innocence is an attribute merely of the want of action *(Nicht-thun)*, a state like the mere being of a stone, and one which is not true even of a child.'[34] This is a far cry from the innocent, desireless action, of *dharma*.

Now we must turn to the idea of innocence in Nietzsche. *Thus Spoke Zarathustra* has been described as 'a new song of "innocence" of cyclic being and becoming'.[35] But this has as its backdrop the terrifying sense of guilt inculcated by Christianity which one may consciously resist and try to counter in a spirit of defiance but cannot ignore or run away from. Therefore *Zarathustra* is not an exercise in non-Christian innocence of the kind that *dharma* makes possible, but is, as Karl Löwith effectively argues, 'from cover to cover a counter-gospel in style as well as in content' conceived 'on the level of Christian "experience"'.[36] Obviously there is a deceptive similarity between Nietzsche's doctrine of eternal recurrence and that pertaining to the cycles of *karma-saṁsāra* and *kalpa* which has misled some scholars in the past. For instance, Alexander Tille in the introduction to his translation of *Zarathustra* likens this doctrine of Neitzsche to the doctrine of Brahmanism and Buddhism.[37] Löwith completely removes the ground for this misunderstanding as he explains that Nietzsche was 'so thoroughly Christian and modern that only one thing preoccupied him: the thought of the future and the will to create',[38] and that he was prevented from achieving innocence through appeal to eternal recurrence by his 'Christian conscience'.[39]

We conclude then that in the Indian sphere of the spirit the problems of ethics as such have been developed without reference to guilt as well as that which springs from it, namely, conscience about conscience, wherein lies its utter distinction from the Western spiritual sphere in this respect. Existential ontology and the moral life have been dissociated and reassociated in a totally different manner and on totally different grounds here. For this one must look to the Vedanta and Buddhism the two dominant religio-philosophical traditions that have had the most decisive influence in shaping Indian spirituality. These two analysed existence, as they did other things, in some ways similarly and in some other ways dissimilarly. But in the phenomenological problem that is at issue here their similarity is all that matters. They are alike in regarding individual existence as a structure of bondage caused by phenomenal consciousness while they are different in their perceptions of the precise modes of its coming into being.

The Vedanta regards phenomenal consciousness as something caused by distortion and mysterious obscuration of one undifferentiated, eternal consciousness identical with Being itself while the Buddhists view it as a self-generating stream sometimes called technically as co-dependent origination *(pratītya-samutpāda)*. The Vedanta in so far as it is a *mīmāṃsā* founded on the Veda does not exhibit to the same degree as does Buddhism that tremendous preoccupation with the intricate processes of becoming. Since it is grounded on the metaphysical Reality of Brahman it sees becoming as a counter-reality, illusory no doubt, and can deal with it somewhat more directly and simply. On the contrary, in Buddhism, as the counter-reality has no admitted ground other than itself, and hence it is what one must start with, it is only by countering it from within with the skill of dialectics that the Reality *(paramārtha-satya)* can be attained. *Nirvāna* is that Reality – of Tranquillity that is – from which all metaphysical considerations must be expelled. Hence *nirvāna* and *saṃsāra* (the stream of becoming) are considered identical; Nāgarjuna the foremost Buddhist dialectician says very explicitly, '*nirvāna* is not different from *saṃsāra* and *saṃsāra* not different from *nirvāna*'.[40] Therefore, the correct knowlege of *saṃsāra* is indispensable for the attainment of *nirvāna*. The agonizing problem for the Buddhist thinkers was, how reliable knowledge was possible within the structure of phenomenal consciousness which is in a state of continual flux.[41]

The manifestation of anxiety through conscience and guilt must lead us to the typical Western/Christian notion of history. Needless to say that our restricted interest does not obligate us to consider the broader questions pertaining to the nature of history as such either in its ontological or methodological aspects. However, it is commonly agreed that history as a discipline in the form of *Weltgeschichte* is Greek in origin while as *Heilsgeschichte* it has its roots in Hebrew religion. The Greek expression of it appears in the form of *theorea* and that must not concern us here. The reigning expression of history governing all aspects of modernity has had its source in the Hebrew-Christian insight. According to the modern view of history as a dimension of Reality with revolutionary implications, it, as Hegel tells us, comes from 'a Hebrew and Christian assumption that history is directed toward an ultimate purpose and governed by the providence of a supreme insight and will'; and the only contribution that (Greek) philosophy has made to it is 'the simple concept of reason' as the 'sovereign of the world'.[42]

However, Löwith calls Hegel the last philosopher of history 'because he is the last philosopher whose immense historical sense was still restrained by the Christian religion'.[43] From Augustine to Hegel a whole line of thinkers interpreted history from a 'centre of meaning' which Löwith mourns has been lost in the modern world. This may or may not be true, but it is significant that one particular interior Christian dimension – although now operating in the world without a centre – seems only to have gained rather than lost in expressive power and vitality; and it must obviously have been there from the beginning of Christianity. In other words, history has become more perceptibly than ever, a structure of anxiety, guilt, over which conscience hovers uneasily and uncannily as a spirit that judges and accuses the whole realm of interconnected events in whose framework social man exists objectively. Where history has weakened in its power of integration it has deepened in pathos and in the sense of tragedy, its diffuseness and centreless- ness themselves being a specific reason.

The formal integration of history with a centre, which Oscar Cullman calls 'the midpoint of the line'[44] structured as *Heilsgeschichte*, achieved by theol- ogy, has had to give way, leaving a big question mark at its centre, in the place of what had formerly been apprehended by faith, making time both in its backward and forward movements a terrifyingly open uncertainty. Yet there is no kind of transvaluation here, which of course cannot under known terms of existence be achieved, because the question mark at the centre is no less internal to the guilt-burdened conscience and anxiety-laden consciousness than the erstwhile object of faith which it has for the most part displaced.

As we turn to the Indian world we perceive that time has no midpoint or centre, either as an object of faith or as a question mark and hence there seems to be no possibility of any dimension of Reality concealed in history forcing its being upon human inwardness. For time is outwardness pure and simple: this can be asserted uniformly of all Indian schools of thought. But no doubt, even in the most idealistic schools, time, along with the rest of phenomena, has an empirical *(vyāvahārika)* reality and this fact cannot be gainsaid. The discipline of gnosis, however, serves the purpose of man's disentangling himself from its web. But religion also provides techniques whereby to live in the world of empirical reality and also to integrate the residuum, which it leaves upon its self-cancelling, with those astringently coherent steps towards liberation. It becomes, therefore, always a means to the ultimate end and within which moral discrimination *(dharma-adharma-vivecana)* is rendered both possible and necessary. Time is even cosmized into mythological world ages and their divisions *(kalpas* and *yugas)* which are conceived to move in repetitive cycles; nevertheless it does not form the basis of history since it is not even a copy of eternity that it is in Plato. Time as either individual life-spans or durations of cosmic ages stands in no relation to eternal Reality whatsoever but only to man's existential situation of being in the process of liberation. This will really cut the ground from under those who hope for a view of history based on the *kalpa* theory.[45]

Dharma

Dharma is truly the Indian counterpart of history that helps to integrate the moral life with the inwardness of tranquillity. If *māyā* (the structure of illusion) implies the principle of dissociation of morality, will and action from the domain of ultimate Reality, *dharma* abides as the principle of their reassociation. However, *dharma* must always preserve its character of innocence, providing no room at all for guilt.

'*Dharma*' which comes from the root *dhr*, meaning to uphold, concerns the moral, social and cosmic orders. The *Mahābhārata* says, 'All human beings are held together by *dharma;* that by which the holding together takes place is called *dharma*.'[46] Such concepts as *kartavya-karma* (duty), *nīti* (customary moral code), *sadācāra* (good conduct), etc., are implications of *dharma*. The ideal society is the *dharma*-society, which embodies innocence and assures the individual of innocent existence while striving for liberation.

Traditionally, the caste itself belongs to this realm of innocence, and hence is not only acceptable but 'good'. All human inequalities are seen as innocent, devoid of guilt, and responsibility for their existence has been removed from men and vested in an intricate mechanism formed by the combination of the three strands of *prakṛti* (nature)[47] and the causal chain of *karma*. Clearly the caste-*dharma*, which is the traditional, innocent ordering of society, can be, and has been at least in the political sphere, replaced by modern egalitarian arrangements, not necessarily due to guilt but by way of seeking newer and more acceptable expressions of the same innocence. However, the traditional as well as the modern will be considered 'just' in its own context because of variable patterns of conformity to *dharma*. Today, Communism itself which had both its birth and nurture in guilt (in the West) is being accepted by some Indians and many other Asians as a new form of innocence. What is true of Communist ideology is also true of technology, which likewise had its origin in the anxiety sphere of the spirit: in the East so far it is being assimilated to tranquillity and innocence. This is also true of certain forms of Christianity itself which do conform to the tranquillity structure as it takes root in the East, which only underscores the point that we made in the previous chapter that revelation as it is grasped not only reshapes but is also in turn reshaped by consciousness.

To be sure *dharma* is also concerned with righting the wrongs of the world but in such a way as it will not affect the structure of innocence, that is, without any implication of self-judgment, accusation or condemnation. But the question is, can there be a genuine impulse to righting the wrongs of the world without the urge to revolution and can there be such an urge without guilt-consciousness? The revolutions that *are* taking place in the East may have to be largely explained as being due to the transmission of ideology through intellectual carriers, and not due to the upsurge of guilt from consciousness.

Righting the wrongs of the world taken seriously must inevitably bring in the inseparable anxiety-conscience-guilt structures of history in the spirit of Hegel's famous dictum '*Die Weltgeschichte ist das Weltgericht*', which has provided the ground for revolutionary ideologies of today. 'Revolutions' that have had the character of innocence, such as the one associated with the name of Mahatma Gandhi, where guiltlessness of all parties, oneself and one's adversaries together, have to be assumed, must exhibit an unavoidable ritual character which, of course, might prove to be surpassingly sane in the long run. But for even this to have been possible some ideological learning, though perhaps without much overt experience of guilt, must have preceded.

Undoubtedly, *dharma* is concerned with the good in the world and in the world to come. It teaches man to discriminate between two contradictory kinds of action, namely, *śubha* (auspicious) and *aśubha* (inauspicious), *puṇya* (meritorious) and *pāpa* (unmeritorious), *kārya* (doable) and *akārya* (non-doable). Hence Kṛṣṇa tells Arjuna in the *Bhagavadgītā*: 'Whenever *dharma* decreases and *adharma* increases I put forth myself. For the rescue of the good and the destruction of the evil-doers, for the consolidation of *dharma*, I come into being (in this world) from age to age.'[48] Asoka, the great emperor who had been converted to the way of the Buddha, published many precepts of *dharma* through his famous edicts. One edict says: 'There is no gift that can equal the gift of Dharma, the establishment of human relations on Dharma, the distribution of wealth through Dharma.'[49] Asoka's empire was reputed for its vigorous implementation of *dharma*. (This does not mean just the Buddhist religion but *dharma* in a more general perspective.) One of the edicts refers to the commissioning of officers charged with responsibility for the establishment and promotion of *dharma* among all religious sects and ethnic groups, nay even among slaves and convicts.[50]

However, the choice between *dharma* and *adharma* is an entirely placid matter. It is based on a natural knowledge, and there is no question here of the kind of predisposition of the will towards evil in spite of, rather than because of, the knowledge of good and evil, so central a Christian idea. In the *dharma* choice there is none of the shattering and consuming terror attendant upon the arrival of such knowledge by eating the fruit of the forbidden tree, a notion that initially and decisively orients Western spirituality towards the opposite pole. In fact, in *dharma* such a knowledge is a very low-key knowledge, conceived to be wholly within human competence to obtain; and the ability to 'act' according to such knowledge is within man's reach, if not always in actuality on account of Nature *(prakṛti* and its constituent *guṇas)*, at least in spirit. Every man must and can cultivate that spirit, for which he needs vigilance, self-control, discrimination, resolution and meditative attention. This is the least common denominator of the messages pertaining to the yoga of action *(karma-yoga)* about which there is a considerable agreement among all schools of interpretation. (Disagreement is notable only with respect to the positive power of *karma* for liberation and its obligatoriness).

To sum up this phase of our inquiry, concern for conscience, guilt, history – these belong together in the anxiety sphere of the spirit; while concern with ontic (becoming) consciousness, along with the means to overcome such consciousness, innocence, *dharma* – these belong together in the tranquillity sphere. Even the awareness of self-identity of religions must obey this pattern of division. Benevolence and tolerance towards other religions and even desire for togetherness must grow from two different stems. Clearly, to know this deep divergence is not thought of as the end of the study, but rather as the indispensable pre-condition for all valid efforts towards profound integration, although never a formal integration, at the deepest levels of consciousness. Such efforts must always be reinforced by the awareness that there is a common Reality in which all men and all religions participate, not, however, in the way they think of it or apprehend it because in the divergence of the spiritual spheres rooted in a phenomenologically grasp-able two-foldness of consciousness it must express itself always as perennial alternatives in respect of truth. This picture constitutes the abiding challenge of religion, and in approaching it we can only go one way, namely, forward. For man cannot say 'no' to an irresistible call of consciousness to transform the polarity of the spheres of the spirit into the mutuality of dialogue. To bring about such mutuality, belongs simply to the creative dimension of thought, quite far removed from discovery.

9

Dialogue

It will have been noticed that the foregoing chapters avoided all metaphysical, theological and mystical issues in comparative religion, choosing to remain on some existential ground only, which then was subjected to comparative phenomenological analysis. In view of that character of this work it will have become self-evidently clear why we should have omitted discussions of a great variety of books in comparative religion, theology, philosophy and mysticism. It will be clear also that in view of the self-limiting character of this study it has had to remain a comparison at a particular level of depth and has had to forbid itself to become a comparison *in extenso* enveloping levels at which such efforts customarily take place having to do with many kinds of details of form and matter of the religions, institutional, cultic, metaphysical, etc.

Wider comparisons such as we have deliberately refused to enter into have indeed their justification. It would be absurd to speak as though between the different worlds of religious experience and thought there is nothing at all that will bear comparison; on the contrary, there is a wide variety of things that are strikingly similar. But our effort has had to be a comparison between two existential centres of consciousness and it has been necessary, accordingly, to depict them in their ultimate mutual distinction, phenomenologically speaking, that is, indeed with no negative purpose in mind at all but with the intention of showing how it would be necessary for the religious thinker of the future to struggle to simultaneously hold the two together.

To force the two spheres asunder in the manner of Indra's separating the sky *(Dyaus)* and the earth *(Prthvī)* prior to creation is really not to reach the terminus of this inquiry but only to prepare the ground for some transcendent integration of the two by bringing about their mutual encompassing in thought. In ordinary acts of comparison at the customary levels some kinds of integration can be achieved. But in comparing the anxiety and the tranquillity structures, the respective existential centres of the two spheres, no such integration is possible; one can only aim at a mutual encompassing, of which the highest moment is dialogue. Such mutual encompassing is conceived because the impossiblity and the utter futility of attempting any formal integration are clearly recognized. Dialogue can only be based on the principle that absolutely different centres – and along with them whole respective spheres – encompass each other. As immediate integration is rejected, as dialogue is apprehended as the real goal, concern for the transcendent integration must express itself in the shape of knowledge of distinction coupled with deep probing of the two spheres.

Although the knowledge of the two spiritual spheres would appear to be the terminus of the investigation, in reality it would reveal itself to be the beginning of a great venture that is signified by man's diverse spiritual history. Such a venture is dialogue. The necessity for dialogue must come from nowhere but the freedom of the human spirit; and that kind of necessity is undoubtedly the greatest of all. For there is no greater compulsion than that which comes from freedom. Dialogue is like religion itself. Hitherto religion has been conceived as an activity grounded in some demonstrable reason. But now in the freedom of thought even the necessity of reason has been transcended. Religion henceforth can be grounded in the necessity of freedom alone. As it has been liberated from all other necessity it must seek its own destiny without any extraneous assistance; this is one of the services of the modern age. In like manner, there is no reason for dialogue to take place unless man in the freedom of his thought freely decides that it should.

DIALOGUE BETWEEN THE RELIGIONS

Dialogue as envisaged here is different in character from that of the so-called dialogue between religions. But in order to see the real difference we must gather knowledge about some of the problems in the latter, although it is in some religious circles an immensely popular theme. This theme is anchored on the thought of the greatest philosopher of dialogue, Martin Buber, to turn to whose teachings would be a natural prerequisite in considering its merits. Buber prophesied:

'A time of genuine religious conversations is beginning – not those so-called but fictitious conversations where none regarded and addressed his partner in reality, but genuine dialogue, speech from certainty to certainty, but also from one openhearted person to another open-hearted person. Only then will genuine common life appear, not that of an identical content of faith which is believed to be found in all religions, but that of the situation of anguish and of expectation.'[1]

Many of the great contemporary religious thinkers have a genuine interest in the dialogue among the religions. The concern for it is expressed powerfully in Tillich, which was the implicit reason for his typological analysis of the religions. He came to the conclusion expressed thus:

'While specific religions as well as cultures do grow and die, the forces which brought them into being, the type-determining elements, belong to the nature of the holy and with it to the nature of man, and with it to the nature of the universe and the revelatory self-manifestation of the divine. Therefore the decisive point in a dialogue between two religions is not the historically determined, contingent embodiments of the typological elements, but those elements themselves.'[2]

In the same manner, Eliade developed his phenomenological position not without an implicit interest in dialogue.[3] Arnold Toynbee, who has great concern with questions of inter-religious relations, has struggled with the issue of the antipathy towards one another among the religions. He discusses this obstinate problem with the sensitivity and urbanity that one has come to expect from him, and offers an eminently civilized solution. However, he makes it appear that what is really involved in dialogue is dealing with difficult people who are driven by prejudices and are bent on being unreasonable. So he writes:

'Since self-centredness is innate in Human Nature, we are all inclined to some extent to assume that our own religion is the only true and right religion; that our own vision of Absolute Reality is the only authentic vision; that we alone have received a revelation; that the truth which has been revealed to us is the whole truth; and that in consequence, we ourselves are 'the chosen people' and 'the children of light' while the rest of the Human Race are gentiles sitting in darkness. Such pride and prejudice are symptoms of Original Sin, and they will therefore be rife in some measure in any human being or community; and the measure varies and it seems to be a matter of historical fact that, hitherto the Judaic religions have been considerably more exclusive-minded than the Indian religions.'[4]

In the light of this noble perspective it must be observed that the difficulty is not altogether man-made as there are in religion itself certain anomalies which come to light only in the religions' attitude towards one another. Mutual aversion, prejudice, and even taboo-making are by no means extraneous or adventitious accretions but paradoxical expressions of inherent essences common to all religions as religions. First of all, all religions must believe that in their revelations the Ultimate Truth is known. But such Ultimate Truth cannot exist unless it is incarnated in some specific forms – and in doing so there inevitably occurs the paradoxical step of particularizing the universal. Surely there is a difference between total incarnation and partial incarnation, as well as between incarnation once and for all and repeatable incarnation, by means of which the universal can be particularized. But we have no grounds for automatically assuming that the less particularized is necessarily truer to the universal as there is a strong possibility that the more particularized ones in their struggle to surpass themselves may often the more urgently desire to rise to, and embody, the universal in the realm of historic actuality. On the other hand, a quiescent universalism must suffer from the absence of the impulse as well as the occasions to realize itself. Hence the spectre of universalism versus particularism that is so frequently presented as though these were attributes of different religions seems to be without foundation.

There is no easy way to bring about openness in religion as it can never be a simple or straightforward achievement. Religions are condemned to maintain loyalty to their own universal truths, more often than not by behaving in a very ununiversalist fashion. The authenticity of religion itself depends upon such loyalty which bespeaks its essentially supra-human, transcendent origin in revelation that no religion can afford to surrender. The courageous student of comparative religion must elicit the truth that is implied in such contradictory manifestations and not be deterred by them.

If, then, openness towards one another is a quality essentially lacking in the religions, because they are religions, *the will to openness* has been added to the character of some religions, most notably Christianity, so that it thenceforth remains, quite militantly, alongside of the *necessary* prohibition against being open. This is the case because dialogue itself has become in these religions a religious category and even a religious *necessity*. The logical integration of these two contradictory kinds of necessity, the perennial and the new, can hardly be achieved, in fact might not even be sought because of the foundation upon freedom of the latter.

When freedom enters the picture, the uniqueness of one religion is maintained by upholding the uniqueness of all. In dialogue, therefore, when we say that one religion is unique, we have to imply that all religions are unique. To the extent that uniqueness is perceived as concrete essence rather than abstract quality the unshare-able has to become share-able. Dialogue, therefore, becomes a matter of shared uniqueness as well as of one uniqueness facing another.

DIALOGUE AS WHAT TAKES PLACE BETWEEN THE SPHERES OF THE SPIRIT

It is quite clear that dialogue itself as a category of religion belongs to one type of religion, namely Judeo-Christian; and it is already at work at both the profound and superficial levels of the religious life today. At the superficial levels it is relatively more effective than at the profound; at the profound levels there is no gauge for measuring its effectiveness, as there can only be grades of authenticity to be tested at the depth of personal thought, despite the fact that it is what takes place *between* persons. But when dialogue is transferred to the domain of relations between two religions, especially when one of them believes in it as a category of religion, while the other does not, it has to be forced back into the depth of consciousness of the person who abides in the hope of it, for whom it is an inescapable necessity grounded in freedom. However, hope must remain hope; by doing so it serves the destiny of that from which it springs.

Even if dialogue is given a place by all religions as a religious category – which is far from being the case – still there are some problems beyond solution. (1) As has been discussed earlier in this essay the essences of all religions lie in some revelation which by definition would make negotiation of it a forbidden contravention of its nature. This would make it absolutely impermissible and impossible to deal with any religion as such and as a whole. (2) Insofar as the religions themselves cannot undertake dialogue but only individuals who are members of them and 'represent' them can, it would be necessary to presuppose that they can grasp, and authoritatively speak for, the whole range of the religions concerned, including most of all the revelatory essences. That would require these individuals to be veritable incarnations of their religions, which surely is beyond the power of human imagination. (3) If it is admitted, as it needs must be, that neither whole religions nor individuals 'representing' them can truly engage in dialogue, it falls to individual persons to effectuate a dialogue within themselves *as if* they represented different religions in their whole range. Now, although under certain spiritual conditions individual thinkers must find it necessary in their freedom to do so, as described above, the limits of such dialogue within must be fully recognized. Freedom is meaningful to man only if he is prepared to use it with awareness of objective limits. Hence it is not possible for a man to be both, say Christian and Buddhist at the same time, even within the range of either being possible for man through participation. But he *can* think Christianity and Buddhism together as an act of freedom, and sometimes he *must*, because to do so is a necessary act of freedom.

Now if we are prepared to move from religions as such and in their whole range, to what is phenomenologically graspable, namely the forms of consciousness cognate with the religions manifested in the spheres of the spirit, dialogue as thinking them together, without the questionable and problematic involvement of the religions and their representatives, can be more easily conceived. Nay, the religious thinker of the future will find that quite inescapable should he desire to know his own freedom. Dialogue, therefore, must be construed as what takes place between the spheres of the spirit in the sense that a thinker thinks them together.

It is necessary, however, to realize that even in dialogue conceived thus the two spheres play two different roles: while the anxiety sphere is marked by its initiative and activity of response, the tranquillity sphere is characterized by silent response and passivity only, to the extent of seeming to be not even awake to the need or the reality of dialogue. The impulse to dialogue itself is of a piece with the essential elements of the former. It is generated by anxiety, and is continuous with guilt, conscience-structure and history. In other words, dialogue between the two spheres takes place by reason of the fact that one of them, the anxiety sphere, has to obey its own nature and therefore seeks to fulfill itself by going beyond itself. But in striving to do so, far from moving about in a vacuum, which it cannot do, it confronts another sphere that is there in fact wherein an alien possibility is recognized to exist in a state of concrete actuality, upon which it confers its character with all the difference it entails but also recoils from it on account of that very fact. Yet the silence and the passivity of that other sphere are also equally important adjuncts for the realization of the self-identity of the anxiety sphere itself and are also absolutely essential factors in the making of dialogue. For, the tranquillity sphere's being there is in itself the chief contribution it makes to dialogue. Undoubtedly, the need to know itself and to know anything else is alien to tranquillity. Hence phenomenology as an intellectual venture, being concerned with self-knowledge and knowledge of another, must come from anxiety alone; but in dialogue the essential silence and passivity of tranquillity will be grasped as a most necessary factor to be incorporated into such an intellectual enterprise *as if* it were active, and to be made to yield the fruits of a truly active agency. Thus it becomes a partnership of a most noble order which one who is bounded within either sphere will scarcely be able to realize whereas one who has heeded the summons to resolutely step out of its boundaries, indeed for no other purpose than to be more fully in it, and cross over to the other, will be privileged at least to taste and to see that it is good. In order to be truly in one's own sphere one has to refuse to be exclusively in it.

In dialogue the immense difference between the two spheres will also be recognized to be the absolute common bond between them; in fact such difference is a far more powerful bond than any kind of similarity. Similarity as such is an occasion for nothing, but polar difference affords the greatest opportunity for the exercise of human freedom by which one can enter deeply into both spheres; and only by entering into both together can one enter into either deeply.

It is most difficult to differ significantly while it is quite easy to resemble non-significantly; there is much to learn from the former and very little from the latter. Hence significant difference is contradiction, and not just contrariety.

Contradiction in the realm of the spiritual life has worried many great minds who have become painfully aware of it and have seriously thought about it, and those burden-bearers have declined the comfort and security of abiding exclusively in the sphere to which they belong. In fact, remaining within the anxiety sphere brings about a certain negative tranquillity that is inherent in it by reason of the felt absence of a significant alternative, but even that is taken away from those who have dared to recognize the existence of the tranquillity sphere, with the result that their anxiety is typically and inexorably accentuated. But such heightened suffering is also a high privilege, as no other necessity than what proceeds from freedom is attached to it. This contradiction between the existential centres of the two spheres of the spirit cannot be dealt with through formal thought, while all other contradictions, metaphysical, logical and historical can at least be subjected to its mediation.

Dialogue, therefore, has no chance of being regarded as working from or towards a formal or material coincidence of opposites. The only coincidence is that which takes place in the mind of the thinker who thinks the contradictory spheres together.

Dialogue requires a common phenomenology of language, which we come to realize does not exist. To be sure, there are metaphysical and logical aspects of the languages used in religion and philosophy in the two spheres which have common elements. Special problems like the relation between language and Reality, language and revelation, and language and meaning can be dealt with in a comparative way just as some common metaphysical problems can be.[5] But they have only a limited usefulness as they only apply to details of method. If, however, such partial or special similarities are regarded in a manner oblivious of the significant divergence between the existential centres of consciousness and their cognate spiritual spheres the result can be very misleading. The essentially non-personal, cyclic, non-phenomenal and unicentric character attached to language in the one sphere must be contrasted with the equally personal, linear, phenomenal and multi-centric character attached to it in the other. These differences have both formal and transformal aspects. The formal ones have come to be counted among the topics of comparative philosophy today like so many other formal topics, but comparisons based on them do not lead to the heart of the matter which must be approached through the comparative phenomenological road, going to the different depths of consciousness.

Phenomenology of language is distinguished by its fundamental problems and its fundamental mode of inquiry; it is concerned with such questions as how does language exist, for whom, and what is the relation between consciousness and language? Therefore, it must be primarily concerned with how we come to be interested in language. It is here that we begin to note some very vital differences. In the Western tradition (bracketing here the logos theory and the Prologue of the Fourth Gospel) the origin of language is traced linearly to a beginning, which could be even before time began. But there must always be a speaker or speakers. Hence philology, which takes us to an original awareness of Reality, perhaps both worldly and divine. This awareness includes self-awareness. To trace the origin of language is to discover the original forms of self-awareness, the achievement of which constitutes self-knowledge. This activity of the mind helps us, as Socrates knew, to move away from the illusion of commonsense and opinion *(doxa)* to the rightness of good sense and knowledge. Socrates knew that words originate in the mutual engagement of man and the world (or in his case more specifically, other men) and he also knew that words tend to become detached and to go off on their own due to human carelessness. The task of philosophy as he conceived it is to cure human thinking of its carelessness. He believed that the original situation of that engagement must be, and can be recalled by the pursuit of words to their origin.

A certain line of continuity of the same concern we see from Socrates to Heidegger. Heidegger's concern for words as part of the *Wortmystik* which alone will help us to 'remember' Being, is surely well-known to scholars. As Allemann tells us: 'He (Heidegger) would *fix* the aggregate of meanings that come into language (in a word), and so would achieve a return through the philosophical speech in all its originality to a precisioning of speech, so that it may fulfil the sharp needs of thinking in the domain of the Being-question.'[6]

This kind of phenomenology of language assumes several things: a linear continuity of language itself, phenomena, person or persons who speak as well as person or persons to whom speech is made, all of which means that speech is made from (and to, in most cases) many centres. The basic mould of speech is time because it is that which assures the progression of centres from which speech can be made. This phenomenological fact is borne out by many clear and convincing instances. We referred to the Prologue of the Fourth Gospel which we, however, bracketed. But take its great statement, 'The Word became flesh'. Here it is to be noted that the point at which the Word *became* flesh is a new centre of utterance, from which Christ could pronounce his famous statement of unity, 'I and my father are one.' Linguistically, this utterance of unity itself is held in a linear frame. This is characteristically different from the statements of the Upaniṣads, 'I am Brahman' *(Aham brahma asmi)*, 'That thou art.' *(Tat tvam asi)*. Now the apparent similarity between Christ's words and the words of the Upaniṣads has misled many, but when we deeply examine them they will prove to be worlds apart, for the former concern the relation of a linear identity between two expressible centres, which must remain two and yet become one, while the latter refer to a retraction of everything that is named 'I' into the one self-same centre, Brahman, for which the movement appropriate is obviously cyclic. The statement 'I and my father are one' is not at odds with the anguished words of Christ in Gethsamene and on the Cross, from which fact we can see that a certain thread of anxiety runs through all of them; on the contrary, the statements of unity of the self and the Supreme Reality that the Upaniṣads contain would be entirely incompatible with anxiety as they indicate only the infinite Reality of tranquillity.

A phenomenology of language and, hence, a phenomenology of religion built on the model of the West, a practice that has been in vogue so far, will not actually serve to explain the corresponding phenomena of the East. A whole line of investigators beginning from Usener and Wilhelm von Humboldt, through Max Müller up to the present have failed to see that a phenomenology of Eastern – or more specifically Indian – religion and religious language could be built only on the particular terms of self-understanding available in that sphere of the spirit itself. In all the important articulations of the phenomenology of religion and language, there is the pervasive hope that a recall of an original situation is possible and once it is done the phenomenon concerned can be fully understood. It is not necessary to say whether it is possible or not possible to do these things, for the error does not lie there at all but in wanting to apply as if without any question whatsoever a Western model, which is undoubtedly true of Western facts of consciousness, to an alien sphere where, as we have briefly demonstrated, it is not applicable.

We have so far isolated and retained the Indian world as the outstanding example of the tranquillity sphere; without it being there as a concrete and self-consistent whole, knowledge of that sphere itself could not have been elicited. Hence it is necessary to continue to abide with it to the very end in our comparative typological study. Insofar as comparative phenomenology

is concerned with the forms of consciousness in both the spheres in our purview, it is vital for a fuller understanding of these forms to incorporate the
types of explanations of phenomena, including and most of all the phenomenon of language,[7] that have been advanced by each. Manifestly, a thorough rewriting of all phenomena, including language itself, in religious
terms had been accomplished before we were introduced to them. In this
too the type difference shows itself very clearly. Such explanations must be
taken seriously in respect of each sphere, and if so phenomenology is bound
to develop in two types concerning these matters too.

DIALOGUE AS WHAT THE THINKER THINKS

Our problem has been to find out what alternative may be said to exist in a
situation in which dialogue in the now classical (as enunciated by Buber[8])
sense is not a realistic possibility. In other words, dialogue between an 'I'
and a 'Thou' (whether these pronouns stand for persons or whole religions
or spheres), insofar as it is an ultimate expression of personal life in the
Western sphere of the spirit, cannot cover the other sphere which operates
in very different terms of the spiritual life, although anxiety concerning the
understanding of it which proceeds from the former must comprehend it,
but only in its own state of passivity and abstention. The I–Thou language
itself is characteristically Western and one of that sphere's profoundest
expressions. So then, let us hear what Buber says:
'The attitude of man is twofold, in accordance with the twofold nature of the
primary words which he speaks. The primary words are not isolated words
but combined words. The one primary word is the combination *I–Thou*.
The other primary word is the combination *I–It*, wherein without a change
in the primary word, one of the words He and She can replace *It*. Hence the
I of the man is also twofold. PRIMARY WORDS DO NOT SIGNIFY THINGS, but
they intimate relations.'
'HERE IS NO *I* TAKEN IN ITSELF, but only the *I* of the primary word *I–Thou*
and the *I* of the primary word *I–It*. When a man says *I* he refers to one or
the other of these.'[9]
Now, however noble in conception, a dialogue between two spiritual
spheres, from the depth of one of which the above view of language comes

while the other has a completely different view of language and of speaking, cannot take place on these terms.

But dialogue as such cannot and must not be surrendered as long as man is capable of thinking. Hence dialogue itself must be removed from the exigencies of inter-personal or inter-religious (or in our case, inter-spherical) relations and be placed in that realm where freedom may be said to exist, albeit only ideally, namely, in the realm of thinking. In Heidegger's words, 'The call (to think) sets our nature free, so decisively that only the Calling which Calls us on to think establishes the free scope of freedom in which free human nature may abide.'[10] Freedom may be said to abide in thinking to the extent that it can contemplate its own limits just as it can contemplate anything else, although by thinking the limits will not be annulled. Heidegger, who elsewhere makes a radical distinction between calculative thinking and meditative thinking and obviously favours the latter as the genuinely human capacity, observes, '[Yet] any one can follow the path of meditative thinking in his own manner and within his own limits. Why? Because man is a *thinking*, that is a *meditating* being. Thus meditative thinking needs by no means be "high-flown". It is enough if we dwell on what lies close and meditate on what is closest....'[11] Yet the dialogue possibility (or as in our terms the thinking together of two different spheres) is commended by Heidegger, for he writes, 'Meditative thinking demands of us not to cling one-sidedly to a single idea, not to run down a one track course of ideas. Meditative thinking demands of us that we engage ourselves with what at first sight does not go together at all.'[12] To this we may add the amendment that the two spheres that we are concerned with do not go together at all, either at first or much later; in fact their essential mutuality consists in their dialectical polarity, making it impossible for either to absorb the other: therein lies an unparallelled potentiality for thought, which must at least now begin to be apprehended.

Why is dialogue as thinking together diverse expressions of Reality preferable to dialogue as what takes place between persons or religions or spheres, although the former too is essentially an expression of the West? The reason primarily is that in the former activity there is no need to count on active responsiveness from quarters where there is no inherent urge to give it or even to be in a state of dialogue; in other words, the passivity and the silence of 'the other' will themselves be turned into a pre-eminent contribution to dialogue. Furthermore, thinking as such, which is universal, goes beyond, and ultimately affects, thinking together (of diverse truths or objects) and in its freedom refuses to be completely object-determined.

The thinker is not alarmed by the constant state of withdrawal in which the tranquillity sphere is encountered. For, it is true, as Heidegger says (concerning whatever is genuinely an object of thought):
'What must be thought about, turns away from man. It withdraws from him. But how can we have the least knowledge of something that withdraws from the beginning, how can we even give it a name? Whatever withdraws refuses arrival. But withdrawing is not nothing. Withdrawal is an event. In fact, what withdraws may even concern and claim man more essentially than anything present that strikes and touches him.'[13]

Heidegger paints a picture of the highest Western ideal of thought (and dialogue) in a way that would be eminently applicable in our inquiry. He writes as follows:
'Once we are so related and drawn to what withdraws, we are drawing into what withdraws, into the enigmatic and therefore, mutable nearness of its appeal. Whenever man is properly drawing that way, he is thinking – even though he may still be far away from what withdraws, even though the withdrawal may remain as veiled as ever. All through his life and right into his death, Socrates did nothing else than place himself into this draft, this current, and maintain himself in it. This is why he is the purest thinker of the West.'[14]

Heinrich Ott undoubtedly reflects Heidegger's mind when he remarks, 'For the situation of dialogue with the other person is a situation I have potentially in myself. Dialogue is not only a possible phenomenon, but rather a basic structure of all existence. Seeking after truth, after understanding, always takes place in dialogue, even when the thinker is alone.'[15]
So then, without in any way rejecting the classic *I–Thou* scheme of dialogue that Buber has given us, the task is to make it dwell in the thinker who thinks and if necessary in his loneliness, where he, taking his place in and with the anxiety sphere, says 'Thou' to the tranquillity sphere after having internalized it through thinking. And if he should deny the power to say 'Thou' likewise to another thinker who takes his place in and with the tranquillity sphere he would be denying the full implication of the 'Thou', which on pain of banishment from truth he must refrain from doing.

Heidegger has exalted the vocation of thought to the highest, and a distinctly religious, level particularly in *Was Heisst Denken?* [What is Called Thinking?]. Heidegger explains that we cannot answer the question, 'What is called thinking?' unless we understand thinking as that to which we are called.[16] In his own words, 'The call endows us with thinking as the dowry of our nature. Through the call, then, man is in a way already informed of what the word 'thinking' means.'[17]

Although thinking together of two polar realities, in other words dialogue, more specifically belongs to the Western sphere of the spirit, thinking as such is common, in fact universal. Heidegger writes:

'However, this word "thinking" as it is sounded in speech, obviously belongs to one particular language. Thinking however, is a matter common to all mankind. Now it is impossible to glean the nature of thinking from the mere signification in one solitary word in one particular language, and then to offer the result as binding. Surely not. The only thing that we can glean that way is that something remains doubtful here. However: the same doubt affects the common, human, logical thinking – provided that henceforth we make up our minds no longer to ignore the fact that all logic, all that belongs to *logos*, is only a single word in the singular and particular language of the Greeks – and not just in its sound structure.'[18]

When we enter thinking we surpass the beginning levels of thinking together of the two, as we will realize that thinking is what belongs to the spheres themselves, and not something essentially imposed on both or either of them by the thinker. Therefore by entering into the spheres deeply the thinker enters into thinking; and there is no other way as thinking in this case means thinking of the two spheres. Also by entering deeply he ceases to think *of* them but thinks *in* them, that is to say specifically, *in* both anxiety and tranquillity and not just *of* them. By thinking *in* them rather than *of* them their abstractness is surpassed and their concreteness established; their remoteness is overcome and they both become immediate, near at hand. They will be seen to be lying close and closest; on them one can meditate.[19]

Also taking the *dia* in dialogue in the sense of 'through' it should be possible for each of the spheres to be the medium for speaking to – and viewing of – the other. Hence even formally speaking, in the place of a logic of disjunction and a logic of alternatives we could have a logic of 'through', that is instead of pvq and p.q, we could have p through q and vice versa.

But ultimately dialogue cannot be spelt out in the language of any formal logic. But then formal logic can lead the way to a contemplative non-choice, which is conceived not as a negative but as a very positive attitude. For the attitude comes from thought itself which calls man from both spheres as it calls him from its own transcendent depth. Thought does not simplify man's task by giving him a choice or by compelling him to be a chooser; and yet the non-chooser is not a syncretist as he sees and speaks from the depth of that in which he is. He is a non-chooser not because he *cannot* choose but because he *can* withstand choosing and do so while contemplating those between which he will not choose. And yet the non-chooser is not a speculative thinker who yearns for Absolute Truth after the Hegelian fashion as though by transcending the partial truths of finite standpoints. The Absolute Truth itself appears to him in a two-fold way insofar as not only what he thinks about but what he thinks *in* are the two spheres of the spirit.

But he fulfils the Hegelian vision of the thinker as the new priest,[20] as he is not only called but also chosen, for it is said that many are called but few are chosen. He is called by thought and is chosen to be a non-chooser in order to perform a specific priestly function of thought. His work which is dialogue is performed not aggressively or violently but walking quietly on the way. To be on the way *('οδος)* [thus] is what after all 'method' *(μεθο-δος)* means. This is the way, roadway, that great thinkers like Parmenides followed. Referring to Parmenides, Werner Jaeger writes:

'Parmenides' 'roadway' *('οδος)* is nowhere to be found on this earth; it is rather the way of salvation, of which he had learned in the mystery religions. Obviously it was here that the concept of the 'way' – innocent enough in itself – first acquired that pregnant significance which it constantly has in Parmenides' writing: the one right way that brings salvation and leads to the goal of knowledge. The philosophical language of a later era was to coin the similar word *μεθοδος*, which also stands for a way to the goal; but how empty, how merely methodical this metaphor seems in comparison with the 'way' of Parmenides, which ... 'leads him who knows unscathed wherever he goes'?'[21]

Heidegger also points out that the essential and abiding element in thought is simply to be on the way. It is therefore, as he adds, a mysterious thing that we can go forward or backward in thought and that above all it is the path backward that leads us forward.[22]

Hence it is necessary that the path backward to the spheres of the spirit and to the ways of consciousness' self-expression in them must be taken so that we be led forward to the goal of knowledge to be achieved in comparative religion. This means that a self-knowledge attained through comparative phenomenology will appear as an essential pre-condition for really fruitful and truthful studies in comparative religion.

Notes and References

NOTES TO 'INTRODUCTION'

1. Louis F. Jordan reports in *Comparative Religion: Its Genesis and Growth* (Edinburgh T. & T. Clark, 1905, p. 181) that the discipline may be dated from 1870, the year in which F. Max Müller 'delivered his memorable lectures on the science of religion at the Royal Institution, London'.
2. *Cf.*, C. R. Haines, *The Communings with Himself of Marcus Aurelius Antoninus* (Cambridge, Mass., Harvard University Press, 1916, Loeb Classical Library, Book VIII), par. 41.
3. *Cf.*, E. Cassirer, *An Essay on Man* (New Haven and London, Yale University Press, 1962), pp. 1–22.
4. *Cf.* Hegel's words: 'The aim of philosophy is to banish indifference and ascertain the necessity of things', William Wallace, *Hegel's Logic*, translated from *The Encyclopaeida of the Philosophical Sciences* (Oxford, Clarendon Press, 1892), p. 222.

NOTES TO 'THE PHILOSOPHICAL SCOPE OF COMPARING IN RELIGION'

1. *Cf.*, Immanuel Kant, *Critique of Pure Reason*, trans. by Norman Kemp Smith (New York, St. Martin's Press; Toronto, MacMillan, 1965), p. 278.
2. *Ibid.*, p. 278.
3. *Cf.*, *Ibid.*, p. 277.
4. *Ibid.*, p. 277.
5. Heidegger observes: '[However], Western thought needed more than 2000 years before the relation with itself (which is present in identity and was hinted already at an earlier date) appeared definitely and well-developed as a process of mediation, before, moreover, men's minds became hospitable to the idea of a manifestation within identity. It was not until the philosophy of speculative idealism made its appearance in Fichte, Schelling and Hegel, after Leibniz and Kant had prepared the way, that the concept of identity whose nature consists in synthesis, met with receptivity.' *Essays in Metaphysics: Identity and Difference*, trans. by Kurt F. Leidecker (New York, Philosophical Library, 1960), p. 15.
6. *Ibid.*, p. 33 ff. In Indian philosophy also identity and difference have been considered

extensively in the *Viśiṣṭādvaita* and the *Bhedābheda* traditions but strictly in respect of onto-theological questions. They can hardly be applied in a phenomenological way.

7. *Cf.*, Kant, *Op. cit.*, p. 279.
8. *Loc. cit.*
9. E. Cassirer, *The Myth of the State* (New Haven and London, Yale University Press, 5th Printing, 1963), p. 7.
10. F. Schleiermacher, *On Religion*, English translation (New York, Harper, 1958).
11. *Cf.*, F. Schleiermacher, *The Christian Faith*, Vol. I. English translation (New York and Evanston, Harper Torchbooks, 1963), p. 48.
12. *Loc. cit.*
13. E. Fackenheim, *The Religious Dimension in Hegel's Thought* (Bloomington and London, Indiana University Press, 1967), p. 9.
14. G. W. F. Hegel, *Lectures on the Philosophy of Religion*, translated from the 2nd German edition by E. B. Spiers and T. B. Sanderson, Vol. I (New York, Humanity's Press, Inc., 1962), p. 19.
15. Kroner's introduction to T. M. Knox and R. Kroner, *On Christianity: Early Theological Writings by Friedrich Hegel*, translation (New York, Harper Torchbooks, 1961), p. 25.
16. Fackenheim, *Op. cit.*, p. 126.
17. Schleiermacher, *The Christian Faith*, I, p. 38.
18. *Cf.*, *Ibid.*, p. 51.
19. *Cf.*, *Ibid.*, p. 52.
20. *Ibid.*, p. 57.
21. *Ibid.*, p. 51. The decisive influence that both romanticism and Spinoza (pantheistic mysticism) exerted on Schleiermacher has been well demonstrated by no less a scholar than Wilhelm Dilthey (see *Das Leben Schleiermachers*, Berlin 1870). In Dilthey's words: 'Schleiermacher's religious activity consisted in finding a respectable place for pantheistic mysticism in the bosom of the Church', here quoted from William Klubach, *Wilhelm Dilthey's Philosophy of History* (New York, Columbia University Press, 1956), p. 77.
22. *Cf.*, *Loc. cit.* Undoubtedly a certain vestige of the Kantian view that all theoretical knowledge is phenomenal and the function of philosophy is to recognize this is still present in this aspect of Schleiermacher's thought, with the crucial difference, however, that it implies the belief that somehow intuition can carry us beyond that point.
23. *Compare:* 'Religion cannot live, says Schleiermacher, without finding expression in traditions and institutions [of this kind] though at the same time all such traditions and institutions are historical products, relative to the age and country which produced them. There is no universal religion, no absolute theology, no universal Church', H. A. Hodges, *The Philosophy of Wilhelm Dilthey* (London, Routledge and Kegan Paul, 1952), p. 11.
24. Schleiermacher, *The Christian Faith*, I, p. 57.
25. T. M. Knox and R. Kroner, *Op. cit.*, p. 15.
26. *Cf.*, *Ibid.*, p. 14.

27. William Wallace, *The Logic of Hegel*, p. 252.

28. *Loc. cit.*

29. *Cf.*, Hegel, *Philosophy of Religion*, Vol. I, p. 336.

30. *Cf.*, *Ibid.*, pp. 328, 335, and *Phenomenology of Mind*, trans. by J. B. Baillie, 2nd edition (London, George Allen & Unwin, Ltd., 6th impression, 1964), pp. 751 ff. etc.

31. *Cf.*, Hegel, *Philosophy of Religion*, Vol. I, pp. 84–85, 327 ff.

32. Hegel, 'Logic 121'. William Wallace, *The Logic of Hegel*, p. 224. This was developed from the earlier doctrine of 'Union of Union and Non-Union', which Richard Kroner described as 'The future philosophical system in a nutshell', T. M. Knox and R. Kroner, *Op. cit.*, p. 14.

33. Wallace, *The Logic of Hegel*, p. 252 ('Logic 139').

34. *Ibid.*, p. 217.

35. *Cf.*, *Ibid.*, p. 216.

36. W. T. Stace, *The Philosophy of Hegel* (London, MacMillan, 1924), p. 509.

37. Fackenheim, *Op. cit.*, p. 23.

38. *Cf.*, *Ibid.*, p. 196, see also p. 193.

39. Wallace, *The Logic of Hegel*, p. 224 ('Logic 121').

40. *Cf.*, T. M. Knox and R. Kroner, *Op. cit.*, p. 31.

41. *Cf.*, Louis H. Jordan, *Op. cit.*, p. 142.

42. See Karl Löwith, *From Hegel to Neitzsche*, trans. by David E. Green (New York, Holt, Rinehart & Winston, 1964).

43. *Cf.*, *Ibid.*, pp. 120 ff.

44. Kierkegaard and Marx are supreme examples of flight from Hegel on the wings of Hegel's dialectics.

45. William James, *A Pluralistic Universe* (London, Longmans, Green & Co., 1909), p. 34.

46. *Cf.*, William James, *The Varieties of Religious Experience* (London, Longmans Green & Co., 23th impression, 1912), p. 430

NOTES TO 'THE ROMANTIC NURSERY OF COMPARATIVE RELIGION AND THE WORK OF MAX MÜLLER'

1. Hegel, *Philosophy of Religion*, Vol. I, p. 89.

2. L. A. Jordan, *Op. cit.*, pp. 63–64.

3. G. E. Lessing, *The Education of the Human Race*, trans. F. W. Robertson, (London, 4th edition, 1883, Harvard Classics, ed. by Charles W. Eliot, Vol. 32. Cambridge, Mass., Harvard University, 1910), p. 195.

4. *Cf.*, *Herders Sammtliche Werke* (Berlin, Weidmannsche Buchhandlung, Band 6, 1883), pp. 288 ff.

5. *Cf.*, Walter Otto, ed., *Die Sprache* (Bayerische Akademie der Schönen Kunste, München, 1949), p. 123.

6. *Cf.*, E. Cassirer, *The Myth of the State*, p. 6.

7. *Cf.*, *Loc. cit.*

8. Max Müller, 'Comparative Mythology', 1856, *Chips From a German Workshop*, Vlo. II (New York, Charles Scribner's Sons, 1881), p. 7.

9. *Cf.*, 'Essays on Language and Literature', 1867, *Collected Works*, Vol. III (London, Longmans Green & Co., 1898), p. 121.

10. *Lectures on The Science of Language*, 1861 (Reprint, Delhi, Munshi Ram Manohar Lal, 1965), p. 387.

11. *Essays on the Science of Religion, Chips from a German Workshop*, Vol. I (New York, Charles Scribner's Sons, 1881), p. ix.

12. *Cf., Loc. cit.*

13. *Ibid.*, pp. 402–403.

14. 'Comparative Mythology', *Chips from a German Workshop*, Vol. II, p. 154.

15. *Science of Language*, p. 403.

16. 'Comparative Mythology', *Chips from a German Workshop*, Vol. II, p. 53.

17. *Loc. cit.*

18. *Ibid.*, pp. 140–141.

19. *Science of Language*, p. 11.

20. 'Comparative Mythology', *Chips from a German Workshop*, Vol. II, p. 16.

21. 'On the Philosophy of Mythology', *Chips from a German Workshop*, Vol. V, p. 68.

22. *Loc. cit.* In a sense Max Müller was essentially reviving Herder's idea of the role of language in the making of myth. Primordial language, accordingly, is the imitation of the living sounds and images of nature, and man the imitator is himself personified myth. Again, in our own time, Walter Otto has reaffirmed this connection between language and myth, see *Die Sprache* (above).

23. *Ibid.*, p. 66.

24. Max Müller writes: 'To one who knows how powerful and important an influence Schelling's mind exercised on Germany at the beginning of this [19th] century, it is hard to say this [his condemnatory remark on Schelling's *Philosophy of Mythology*]. But if we could read his posthumous volume [the above work] without sadness, and without a strong feeling of the mortality of all human knowledge, we cannot mention them, [Schelling's thoughts] when they must be mentioned, without expressing our conviction that though they are interesting on account of their author, they are disappointing in every respect,' in 'Greek Mythology', *Chips from a German Workshop*, Vol. II, p. 144.

25. 'On the Philosophy of Mythology', *Chips from a German Workshop*, Vol. V, p. 66.

26. 'Comparative Mythology', *Chips from a German Workshop*, Vol. II, p. 10.

27. *Cf. Science of Language*, p. 246.

28. 'Philosophy of Mythology', *Chips from a German Workshop*, Vol. V, p. 92.

29. *Introduction to the Science of Religion* (First Lecture), (London, Longmans Green & Co., 1873), p. 12.

30. 'Address to the International Congress of Orientalists, 1874', *Chips from a German Workshop*, Vol. IV, p. 327.

31. The lectures were delivered in Westminster Abbey in April, May, June, 1878; the volume has been reprinted at Varanasi by the Indological Book House in 1964.

32. *Essays on the Science of Religion, Chips from a German Workshop*, Vol. I, p. x.
33. *Loc. cit.*
34. *Ibid.*, p. xi.
35. 'Address to the International Congress of Orientalists', *Chips from a German Workshop*, Vol. IV, p. 328.
36. *Ibid.*, p. 325.
37. *Cf. Loc. cit.*
38. *Cf. Introduction to the Science of Religion*, p. 67.
39. *Cf.*, Knox and Kroner, *Op. cit.* (Introduction), p. 15.
40. Max Müller's barb against Hegel in this respect (*Essays on the Science of Religion*, p. ix) is, again, a reflection of his inability to understand great philosophers.
41. 'Address to the International Congress of Orientalists, 1874', *Chips from a German Workshop*, Vol. IV, pp. 326–327.

NOTES TO 'COMPARATIVE RELIGION AS HISTORY OF RELIGION AND THE QUEST FOR HISTORICAL SELF-KNOWLEDGE'

1. *Cf.*, H. A. Hodges, *The Philosophy of Wilhelm Dilthey, Op. cit.*, p. 236. See also, W. Dilthey, *Gesammelte Schriften* (Leipzig, Teubner, 1914–65), Vol. V, pp. 309–316.
2. *Cf.*, *Ibid.*, pp. 169 ff. See also *Gesammelte Schriften*, Vol. VII, pp. 159–169.
3. *Ibid.*, p. 259. See also *Gesammelte Schriften*, Vol. VII, pp. 120–129.
4. *Ibid.*, pp. 262–263. See also *Gesammelte Schriften*, Vol. VII, pp. 143–146.
5. Cornelius Tiele, *Elements of the Science of Religion*, (Edinburgh, 1897–9), Vol. I, p. 17.
6. This problem was of great interest to Joachim Wach. See his book, *The Comparative Study of Religions*, ed. by Joseph Kitagawa (New York and London, Columbia University Press, 1958), Ch. I; also *Einleitung in die Religionssoziologie* (Tübingen, Mohr, 1930); *Religionswissenschaft, Prolegomena zu ihrer Grundlegung* (Leipzig, Hinrichs, 1924).
7. *Cf.*, Hodges, *Op. cit.*, p. 265.
8. Ludwig Feuerbach, *Lectures on the Essence of Religion*, trans. by Ralph Mannheim (New York, Harper and Row, 1967), p. 23.
9. *Cf.*, *Loc. cit.*
10. *Cf.*, *Loc. cit.*
11. *Loc. cit.*
12. Socrates himself grappled with this issue existentially, that is, as a problem concerning himself rather than as a problem in general, and resolved it through the philosophical method of ignorance. 'What made Socrates free was that in non-knowledge he had certainty of the goal towards which he had undertaken the venture of his life and now of his death,' Karl Jaspers, *Socrates, Buddha, Confucius, Jesus*, ed. by Hannah Arendt (New York, Harcourt, Brace and World, Inc. 1962), p. 15.
13. In Western thought the relations between the two, self-knowledge and revelation, have never been truly resolved, partly owing to their diverse origins. However far the two

are produced they behave like parallel lines that never meet. In Indian thought, since their source is the same, they originated in an indivisible unity.

14. Compare Karl Barth who writes describing the real self-knower, 'For it is precisely the man who is placed in the real knowledge of the Word of God who recognizes himself as completely existing in his self-determination', *Church Dogmatics*, Vol. I, part I, translated by G. T. Thomson (Edinburgh, T. & T. Clark, 1936), p. 229.

15. *Cf.*, *The Bṛhadāraṇyaka Upaniṣad*, IV, 4.22.

16. *Cf.*, *The Chāndogya Upaniṣad*, VI.

17. S. Radhakrishnan (editor and translator), *The Principal Upaniṣads* (London, George Allen & Unwin, 1953), p. 619.

    nāyam ātmā pravacanena labhyo na medhayā, na bahunā śrutena:
    yamevaiṣa vṛnute, tena labhyas tasyaiṣa ātmā vivṛnute tanūm svām.

NOTES TO 'SOME PHENEMENOLOGICAL THEORIES OF RELIGION'

1. *Cf.*, G. van der Leeuw, 'History of Phenomenological Research', Appendix to *Religion in Essence and Manifestation*, trans. by J. E. Turner (New York and Evanston, Harper Torchbooks, 1963), Vol. II, p. 690.

2. One readily thinks of the Jungians.

3. E. Cassirer's *Philosophy of Symbolic Forms* is still the classic expression of the thought implied here.

4. Kant, *Critique of Pure Reason*, trans. by Norman Kemp Smith, p. 276.

5. Rudolf Otto, *The Idea of the Holy*, trans. by John Harvey (New York, Oxford University Press, 1961), Galaxy, p. 7

6. *Cf.*, *Loc. cit.*

7. *Cf.*, *Ibid.*, p. 11.

8. *Cf.*, *Loc. cit.*

9. *Cf.*, *Ibid.*, p. 10.

10. *Cf.*, *Ibid.*, p. 5.

11. *Cf.*, van der Leeuw, *Op. cit.*, p. 677.

12. *Cf.*, *Ibid.*, pp. 671, 672, etc.

13. *Cf.*, *Ibid.*, p. 671.

14. *Cf.*, *Ibid.*, p. 672.

15. *Ibid.*, p. 672.

16. *Ibid.*, p. 673.

17. *Cf.*, *Ibid.*, p. 677.

18. *Cf.*, *Ibid.*, p. 676.

19. *Ibid.*, pp. 675–676. See also Max Scheler, *Die Stellung des Menschen in Kosmos* (63), 1928; also Heidegger, *Sein und Zeit*, p. 38.

20. Karl Jaspers, *Truth and Symbol*, trans. from *Von der Wahrheit*, by Jean T. Wilde, William Kluback and William Kimmel (New York, Twayne Publishers, 1947), p. 37.

21. Van der Leeuw, *Op. cit.*, p. 683.

22. *Cf.*, *Ibid.*, p. 684.
23. *Cf.*, *Ibid.*, p. 679.
24. *Cf.*, *Ibid.*, p. 681.
25. *Cf.*, *Ibid.*, p. 683.
26. *Cf.*, *Loc. cit.*
27. *Ibid.*, pp. 683–684.
28. Mircea Eliade, *Yoga, Immortality and Freedom*, trans. by Willard R. Tarsk (New York, Pantheon Books, Inc., published for the Bollingen Foundation, 1958), p. xix.
29. *Cf.*, Mircea Eliade, *Cosmos and History: The Myth of the Eternal Return*, trans. by Willard R. Tarsk (New York, Harper and Row, Harper Torchbooks, 1959), p. 142.
30. *Cf.*, *Ibid.*, p. 149.
31. *Cf.*, *Ibid.*, p. 153.
32. *Cf.*, *Ibid.*, p. 162.
33. *Cf.*, *Yoga, Immortality and Freedom*, p. 361.
34. *Cf.*, *Ibid.*, pp. 361–362.
35. *Cf.*, *Ibid.*, p. 364.
36. *Cf.*, *Cosmos and History*, p. 161.
37. *Ibid.*, pp. 161–162.
38. *Yoga, Immortality and Freedom*, p. xix.
39. Heidegger observes, 'Reason and its conceptions are only one kind of thinking and are by no means determined by themselves but by that which is called thinking, to think in the manner of the *ratio*', *The Question of Being*, trans. by William Kluback and Jean T. Wilde, (New York, Twayne Publishers Inc., 1956), p. 39.
40. E. Cassirer, *An Essay on Man*, p. 25.
41. Nietzsche is one 'insane' philosopher who *saw* the anxiety of modern man as very few moderns could. As Karl Jaspers writes, 'Nietzsche undertakes to grasp contemporary nihilism historically. But this age does not even know what is happening to it, let alone *where* its situation originated. Nietzsche lives with the horror of seeing what no one sees and of knowing what no one else worries about: The event "is so huge . . . that one may scarcely maintain that even intelligence of it has already arrived – to say nothing of a general awareness of its implications and of a realization of how much must collapse once this faith is undermined, because it . . . was built on it".' *Nietzsche*, trans. by Charles F. Wallroft and Frederick J. Schmitz (Tuscon, University of Arizona Press, 1965), p. 244.

NOTES TO 'CONSCIOUSNESS AND RELIGION'

1. *Cf.*, Edmund Husserl, *Ideas*, trans. by W. R. Boyce Gibson (New York, Collier Books, 1962), pp. 103–104; See also *Ideen zu einer Reinen Phänomenologie und phänomeno-logischen Philosophie*, Book I (The Hague, Martinus Nijhoff, 1950), pp. 74–76.
2. *Ibid.*, p. 102; see *Ideen*, I, p. 72.
3. *Ibid.*, p. 200; see *Ideen*, I, p. 181.

4. *Cf.*, *Ibid.*, pp. 202–203; see also *Ideen*, I, pp. 182–183. *Cf.*, *The Phenomenology of Internal Time Consciousness*, ed. by Martin Heidegger, trans. by J. S. Churchill (Bloomington, Indiana University Press, 1966), particularly Appendix IX, entitled 'Primal Consciousness and possibility of reflexion'.

5. *Ibid.*, p. 201; see *Ideen*, I, pp. 181–182.

6. *Cf.*, *Sein und Zeit*, Tübingen edition (Tübingen, Max Niemeyer, 1953), p. 31.

7. *Cf.*, *Ibid.*, p. 35.

8. *Ideas*, p. 103; see also *Ideen*, I, p. 74.

9. *Ibid.*, p. 104; see also *Ideen*, I, p. 75.

10. Husserl writes, '[On the contrary], the transition to pure consciousness through the method of transcendental reduction leads necessarily to the ground of what presents it as the intuitable actuality *(Factizität)* of the corresponding constituting consciousness. It is not concrete actuality *(Faktum)* in general, but concrete actuality as the source of possible and real values extending infinitely, which compels us to ask after the 'ground' which of course has not then the meaning of a substance', *Ideas*, p. 158; see *Ideen*, I, pp. 138–139.

11. *Ibid.*, p. 155. *Ideen*, I, pp. 136–137.

12. It is perhaps Karl Ottfried Müller (in *Prolegomena zu einer Wissenschaftigen Mythologie*, Göttingen, 1825) who first put forward the theory that myth originates in the people *(das Volk)*, rather than in the minds of gifted individuals or priests, as Creuzer had thought. What is true of myths in general must be true of myths representing the sense of wrongness.

13. *Cf.*, Paul Elmer More, *The Sceptical Approach to Religion* (Princeton, Princeton University Press, 1934), p. 4.

14. Martin P. Nilsson, *Religion as a Protest Against the Meaninglessness of Events* (Lund, C. W. K. Gleerup Publishers, 1954), p. 26.

15. There is much in the literature of religion and of anthropology which will corroborate Nilsson's view. One only needs to look at some of the chapter headings of Paul Radin, *The Primitive Man as Philosopher* (New York, Dover, 1957), for example, 'Fate, Death and Resignation' (Ch. VIII); 'The Tragic Sense of Life' (Ch. XI). Radin quotes a number of primitive poems in which 'the whole gamut is run from mild complaint to denunciation'. p. 15. We may also note B. Malinowski's work, *Magic, Science and Religion*, among many others. 'The Gilgamesh Epic' has also been frequently described as 'revolt against death'. See, Cornelius Loew, *Myth, Sacred History and Philosophy*, (New York, Harcourt, Brace & World, Inc., 1967). The idea of Fate itself is a protest against death.

16. *Isaiah* 53.4 (King James Version).

17. There is a partial similarity between our understanding of images and Karl Jaspers' as he deals with them as cyphers. But the similarity stops when Jaspers begins to describe cyphers as Being itself and when he begins to indicate the path of transcendence through them. See Karl Jaspers, *Truth and Symbol*, pp. 57–59.

18. *Cf.*, Susan A. Taubes, 'The Absent God', included in J. J. Altizer, ed., *Toward a New Christianity* (New York, Harcourt, Brace and World, Inc., 1967), p. 11.

19. Heidegger, it appears, insists on excluding the otherness of the other in his notion of the *Seiende*, but also insists on 'letting *Seiende* be what it is'. See *Vom Wesen der Wahrheit*. But he argues, nevertheless, that *Seiende* be admitted to the transcendental horizon in order to find a ground, while on the other hand the possibility of the horizon is grounded in the *Seiende*. See *Vom Wesen des Grundes*. But some theologians of a decade ago criticized him on this score as they felt that he had refused to complete the logical circle in his argument in respect of letting *Seiende* be what it is and if he had done otherwise he would have both removed the possibility of 'arbitrariness' and 'subjectivism' and would have made room for the actuality of the other as the other. See Thomas Langman, *The Meaning of Heidegger* (London, Routledge and Kegan Paul, 1959), p. 228.

20. *Cf.*, Merlau-Ponty writes, 'Since God is truth, I always serve Him in saying what I think, on the sole condition that I have done my utmost to clarify my ideas', *Sense and Non-sense*, English trans. by H. L. Dreyfus and P. A. Dreyfus (Evanston, Ill., North-Western University Press, 1964), p. 174. See also, Eugen Fink, *Zur ontologischen Frühgeschichte von Raum, Zeit, Bewegung* (The Hague, Nijhoff, 1957), pp. 141–142.

21. *Cf.*, *Sein und Zeit*, 63, pp. 310–316; trans. by Macquarrie *(Being and Time)*, pp. 358–364. 'Where does this [existential] interpretation get its clue, if not from an idea of existence in general which has been "presupposed"?', *Being and Time*, p. 361.

22. *Cf.*, Walter F. Otto, *Die Gestalt und das Sein* (Darmstadt, Wissenschaftliche Buchgesellschaft, 1959), p. 224; see also Vincent A. Vycinas, *Earth and the Gods: An Introduction to the Philosophy of Martin Heidegger* (The Hague, Nijhoff, 1961).

23. Paul Ricœur, *The Symbolism of Evil*, trans. by Emerson Buchanan (New York, Harper and Row, 1967), p. 4.

24. This is the central thesis of his book, *Fallible Man: Philosophy of the Will*, trans. by Charles Kelbley (Chicago, Henry Regnery Co., 1965).

25. *Ibid.*, p. 3.

26. *The Symbolism of Evil*, p. 357.

27. *Ibid.*, p. 22.

NOTES TO 'ANXIETY AND TRANQUILLITY: THE SPHERES OF THE SPIRIT'

1. Paul Tillich, *Christianity and the Encounter of the World Religions* (New York, Columbia University Press, 1961), p. 54.

2. Walter Otto, *The Homeric Gods*, trans. by Moses Hadas (Boston, Beacon Press, 1964), p. 5.

3. *Epistle to the Romans*, 8: 22, 23.

4. *The Māndūkya Upaniṣad*, 7.

5. *The Maitrī Upaniṣad*, VII. 3.

6. See also *The Maitrī Upaniṣad* VI. 31, and VII. 4.

7. *Sarvam khalu idam brahma tajjalān iti śānta upāsīta*, *The Chāndogya Upaniṣad*, III. 14. 1a.

8. *Śāntatvam yogābhyāsāt āpnoti*, The Maitrī Upaniṣad VI. 29.

9. T. R. V. Murti exemplifies this when he forcefully argues that no school of Buddhism ever took *nirvāṇa* as nothing 'but as an *asaṁskṛta dharma*, a sort of noumenal unconditioned reality behind the play of phenomena', *The Central Philosophy of Buddhism* (London, George Allen & Unwin, 1955, 3rd impression 1970), p. 272.

10. *Cf.*, *Mādhyamika kārikā vṛtti* of Candrakirti, quoted by Murti, *Op. cit.*, p. 274.

11. *Cf.*, *Sein und Zeit*, p. 177; *Being and Time*, p. 222.

12. *Cf.*, *The Bhagavadgītā*, XVI. One is supposed to cut off this tree with the powerful sword of non-association *(asaṅga-śastreṇa)*, *Ibid.* XV. 3, or the sword of knowledge *(jñāna-paramāsinā)*, *The Mahābhārata*, *Aśvamedhaparva*, 47.12–15.

13. *Cf.*, Paul Tillich, *Systematic Theology*, Vol. I, (Chicago, University of Chicago Press, 1951), p. 191.

14. *Cf.*, S. Kierkegaard, *The Sickness Unto Death*, trans. by Walter Lowrie (Princeton, Princeton University Press, 1944), p. 44.

15. *Ibid.*, pp. 43–44.

16. *Ibid.*, p. 44. *Compare:* 'Existence is the child that is born of the infinite and the finite, the eternal and the temporal, and is therefore a constant striving', Kierkegaard, *Concluding Unscientific Postscript*, trans. by Walter Lowrie (Princeton, Princeton University Press, 6th impression, 1960), p. 85.

17. The negative form of relation, namely disrelation, is as important in Heidegger as in Kierkegaard insofar as it is revelatory of the Self's possiblity. Laszlo Versényi observes quite correctly, 'As in the biblical view of man, he *(Dasein)* can have a negative relation to God (in sin) while at the same time it is impossible for him, whose essence lies in his God-relationship, not to be related to God at all, so in Heidegger's view of existence there is a deficient mode of 'being ontological' but not to be ontological at all is impossible to Dasein, whose essence lies in its existence, i.e., in its concern about Being', *Heidegger, Being and Truth* (New Haven and London, Yale University Press, 1965), p. 10.

18. Tillich, *Systematic Theology*, Vol. I, p. 191.

19. *Cf.*, Versényi, *Op. cit.*, p. 15.

20. *Loc. cit.*

21. Kierkegaard, *Concluding Unscientific Postscript*, p. 182.

22. *Psalm* 98: 4–8.

23. From *The Confessions of St. Augustine*, quoted from Roger Hazelton, ed., *Selected Writings of St. Augustine* (Cleveland and New York, The World Publishing Company, Meridian Books, 1963), p. 29.

24. From the *Koran*, trans. by J. M. Rodwell (London, Everyman's Library, 1963, reprint), Sura VIII.

25. *Ibid.*, Sura LXV.

26. *Cf.*, *Sein und Zeit*, p. 137; *Being and Time*, p. 176.

27. *Cf.*, *Ibid.*, p. 135; *Being and Time*, p. 174.

28. *Cf.*, *Ibid.*, p. 175; *Being and Time*, pp. 219–220.

29. *Cf.*, *Loc. cit.*

30. J. M. Robinson, 'The German Discussion', Robinson and Cobb, *Op. cit.*, p. 39. See Heidegger, *Was ist Metaphysik?* (Frankfurt, A. M. Vittorio Klastermann, 1960, 8th edition), p. 49, and also *Existence and Being*, trans. by R. C. Hull and A. Crick (London, Vision Press, 1949) p. 389; (Chicago, Henry Regnery Co., 1960), p. 358. The same point is elaborated by Robinson in 'Heilsgeschichte and Lichtungsge-schichte', *Evangelische Theologie*, XXII, 1962, and later in 'Historicality of Biblical Language', in B. W. Anderson, ed., *The Relevance of the Old Testament for the Christian Faith.*
31. *Cosmos and History*, p. 162.
32. See particularly 'Die Frage nach der Technik', *Vorträge und Aufsätze* (Pfullingen, 1954).
33. *Cf.*, Robinson and Cobb, *Op. cit.*, p. 29.
34. *Viṣṇu-sahasranāma (The Mahābhārata, Anuśāsana Parva)*. See ed. by R. Ananta-krishna Sastry, with the commentary of Śankara (Adyar, Madras, Theosophical Publishing House, 1927), pp. 33, 34.
35. *Ibid.*, p. 18.
36. *Dhammapāda*, 380A.
37. *Cf.*, Walter Otto, *Op. cit.*, p. 7.
38. *Ibid.*, p. 263.
39. *Cf., Ibid.*, p. 264.
40. *Ibid.*, p. 265.
41. *Ibid.*, p. 284.
42. Ecstasy's connection with Shamanism has been asserted by students of primitive religion in the sense of *enthousiasmos*, the state of being filled with God. (See Karl Jaspers, *Psychologie der Weltanschauungen*). As *enthousiasmos* it is important for Plato (*Symposium* 218), who, however, modifies it as love of wisdom. Paul Tillich is one of the modern writers gripped by the idea of ecstasy, who correlates it with miracle (*Systematic Theology*, Vol. I, pp. 111 ff.). 'Ecstasy (standing outside oneself [ek-stasis],' he writes, 'points to a state of mind which is extraordinary in the sense that it transcends ordinary situations. Ecstasy is not a state of mind in which reason is beyond itself, that is, its subject-object structure.' Heidegger uses 'ek-stasis' or 'extasis' frequently as it has the same importance as 'ek-sistenz' itself, where the usage although ontological does not convey the kind of meaning that 'ecstasy' has in association with fortuitousness of being that we are able to perceive in that line of special development from polytheism, but in reality seems inclined towards the idea of gratuitousness.
43. *The Br̥hadāraṇyaka Upaniṣad*, II. 1.20.
44. *The Bhagavadgītā*, II. 51.
45. *The Īśā Upaniṣad*, 15.
46. Heidegger refers to the 'active nihilism' of Nietzsche where 'the action of the work consisted – and in a changed function still consists – in the fact that it makes the "total work character" of all reality visible from the figure of the worker', *The Question of Being*, trans. by William Kluback and Jean T. Wilde, (New York, Twayne Publishers Inc., 1956), p. 41.

47. *Concluding Unscientific Postscript*, p. 51.
48. *Cf.*, Karl Jaspers, *Nietzsche*, p. 435.
49. *Ibid.*, pp. 435–436.
50. *Cf.*, T. R. V. Murti, *Op. cit.*, p. 333. In fact to correct this one-sided negative view of *śūnyata* and *nirvāna* is the major purpose of Murti's excellent work.

NOTES TO 'ANXIETY AND TRANQUILLITY: SOME ASSOCIATED NOTIONS'

1. *Concluding Unscientific Postscript*, p. 264, footnote.
2. *Ibid.*, p. 188.
3. *Loc. cit.* However, Kierkegaard leaves only as implicit the idea that it is faith itself that makes the infinite depth of anxiety a possibility to be grasped symbolically rather than as an actuality. Further, by presenting the category of *the absurd* as the decisive one by reason of the 'paradoxicality of the paradox', he seems to place the premium, quite contrary to his intention no doubt, on the formally logical aspect of the problem.
4. Paul Tillich, *The Protestant Era* (Chicago, University of Chicago Press, 1948), p. 137.
5. *Cf., Ibid.*, p. 137.
6. *Epistle to the Romans* 2: 14–15.
7. *Cf.*, W. E. Gladstone, ed., *Bishop Butler*, Vol. II (Oxford, Clarendon Press, 1896), par. 7 and 8.
8. *Cf.*, Kant, *Critique of Practical Reason* and other works, ed. and trans. by T. K. Abbot (London, Longmans, 1927), pp. 321 ff.
9. *Cf.*, Hegel, *Phenomenology*, p. 668.
10. *Loc. cit.*
11. *Loc. cit.*
12. *Ibid.*, p. 644.
13. *Cf., The Genealogy of Morals*, quoted by Tillich, *The Protestant Era*, p. 147.
14. *Ibid.*, pp. 137–138.
15. This is the subject matter of *Sein und Zeit*, 55–60.
16. *Cf., Ibid.*, p. 275; *Being and Time*, p. 320.
17. *Cf., Being and Time*, p. 32; *Sein und Zeit*, p. 275.
18. *Loc. cit.*
19. *Ibid.*, p. 321; *Sein und Zeit*, p. 276.
20. Hegel, *Phenomenology*, p. 654.
21. *Cf., Ibid.*, p. 649.
22. *The Protestant Era*, p. 145.
23. From *King Richard III*, Act V, Scene III.
24. *The Protestant Era*, p. 138. *Cf.*, also John Macquarrie, *An Existentialist Theology* (London, S.C.M. Press, 1955), p. 143.
25. Hegel, *Phenomenology*, p. 488.
26. *Being and Time*, p. 334; *Sein und Zeit*, p. 288.
27. *Cf., Ibid.*, p. 332; *Sein und Zeit*, p. 286.

28. Susil Kumar Maitra, *The Ethics of the Hindus* (Calcutta, University of Calcutta Press, 1963), p. 110.
29. *Ibid.*, p. 114.
30. *Cf., Loc. cit.*
31. See Kierkegaard, *The Concept of Dread*, trans. by Walter Lowrie (Princeton, Princeton University Press, 1944), pp. 37 ff.
32. *The Bhagavadgītā*, V. 12.
33. *Ibid.*, VI. 3.
34. Hegel, *Phenomenology*, p. 488.
35. *Cf.*, Karl Löwith, *Meaning in History* (Chicago, University of Chicago Press, Phoenix Books, 7th impression, 1962), Appendix II, 'Nietzsche', p. 220.
36. *Cf., Loc. cit.*
37. Nietzsche, *Thus Spake Zarathustra*, trans. by Alexander Tille (London, T. Fisher Unwin, 1908), p. xiv.
39. *Cf.*, Löwith, *Meaning in History*, p. 221.
38. *Cf., Loc. cit.*
40. *Na saṁsārasya nirvānāt kiṁcid asti viśeṣaṇam*
    Na nirvānasya saṁsārat kiṁcid asti viśeṣaṇam,
    Mādhyamikakārikā, XXV, 19.
41. See Theodore Stcherbatsky, *The Central Conception of Buddhism* (Calcutta, Susil Gupta, reprint 1961), p. 45 ff.
42. *Cf.*, Karl Löwith, *Meaning in History*, p. 54.
43. *Cf., Ibid.*, p. 57.
44. Oscar Cullmann, *Christ and Time*, trans. by Floyd V. Filson (London, S.C.M. Press, reprint 1957), p. 105.
45. Eliade mentions such a possibility although he recognizes the 'Indian refusal of history', see *Cosmos and History*, p. 117.
46. The *Mahābhārata*, *Karnaparva*, 69.50.
47. The three strands or *gunas*, classically analysed in the Sānkhya system, are *satva* (goodness), *rajas* (energy) and *tamas* (darkness).
48. *The Bhagavadgītā*, IV. 7,8.
49. N. A. Nikam and Richard McKeon, *The Edicts of Asoka* (Chicago, University of Chicago Press, 1959), p. 44.
50. *Cf., Ibid.*, pp. 38, 59.

Notes to 'Dialogue'

1. Martin Buber, *Between Man and Man*, trans. by Ronald Gregor Smith (Boston, Beacon Press, 5th printing, 1961), pp. 6–7.
2. *Christianity and the Encounter of the World Religions*, p. 57.
3. See *Yoga, Immortality and Freedom*, p. xx; *Cosmos and History*, p. 159.

4. Arnold Toynbee, *An Historian's Approach to Religion* (London, Oxford University Press, Geoffrey Cumberledge, 1957), p. 284.
5. See as an example the author's own 'Language and Knowledge: A Vedantic Examination of a Barthian Issue', *Union Seminary Quarterly Review*, (New York), XXV (2), Winter 1970.
6. B. Allemann, *Hölderlin und Heidegger*, quoted from Thomas Langman, *The Meaning of Heidegger*, p. 114.
7. This problem has been dealt with by the author in 'Language and Phenomena', *Canadian Journal of Theology* (Toronto), XVI (1–2), 1970.
8. Martin Buber, *I and Thou*, trans. by Ronald Gregor Smith, (New York, Charles Scribner's Sons, 1958).
9. *Ibid.*, pp. 3–4.
10. Martin Heidegger, *Was Heisst Denken?* Translation *What is Called Thinking?* by Fred D. Wieck and J. Glenn Gray (New York, Harper & Row, 1968 – 'Religious Perspectives', 23), pp. 132–133.
11. Martin Heidegger, *Discourse on Thinking*, trans. by John M. Anderson and E. Hans Freund (New York, Harper & Row, 1966), p. 53.
12. *Loc. cit.*
13. *What is Called Thinking?*, pp. 8–9.
14. *Ibid.*, p. 17.
15. Heinrich Ott, 'What is Systematic Theology?', Robinson and Cobb, *Op. cit.*, p. 96.
16. *Cf. What is Called Thinking?*, pp. 132–133.
17. *Ibid.*, p. 132.
18. *Ibid.*, p. 133.
19. *Cf.*, Heidegger, *Discourse on Thinking*, p. 53. (See *supra*).
20. See Fackenheim, *op. cit.*, p. 235.
21. *The Theology of the Early Greek Philosophers* (Oxford, Clarendon Press, 1947), p. 98.
22. 'Das Bleibende im Denken ist der Weg. Und Denkwege bergen in sich das Geheimnisvolle, dass wir sie vorwärts und rückwärts gehen können, dass sogar der Weg zurück uns erst vorwärts führt', M. Heidegger, *Unterwegs zur Sprache* (Tübingen, Neske, 1960), p. 99.

Index of Names

Index of Subjects